For What We Are About to Receive

Recipes from GLENDA GORDON BARRIE

New and Enlarged Edition

For What
We Are
About To
Receive

Glenda Gordon Barrie

Second edition

Copyright (c) 2016 by Glenda Gordon Barrie

Printed by For the Right Reasons,
60 Grant Street,
Inverness, IV3 8BS

Contents

3

Acknowledgements

With fond memories and thanks to all those at Gavins:-

Gavin Barlow & Nick Taylor, Suzie Moir, Suzie Dendy, Belles, Tiffany, Nadia, Miranda, Annie, Monika, Brenda, Carrie, Doreen, Marianne, Gail, Kevin, Ian, Peter, Gordon and Jeannie.

I am delighted that this book is to be published by the Reverend Richard Burkitt of "For the Right Reasons". He and his team do an impressive job by helping and supporting people in the area to free themselves from drug and alcohol addiction. They are given work, encouragement, friendship and counselling to stay clean and live a better life.

My thanks go to Lady (Nicola) Irwin, who initiated the idea that I write a recipe book to raise funds for St Margaret's Church, Aberlour, and to Lynette and Angus Findlay, who have supported and encouraged me. They also generously took over the typing.

Thanks to Tricia Lawson for photography and to Lindsay MacGregor and Olive Findlay for illustrations.

Introduction

An interest in food and cooking came to me rather late, in fact not until 1961 when I was in my early twenties and I joined British Overseas Airways as a stewardess. We were given an intensive eight week trainings course covering all aspects of the job. A doctor instructed us on our general health and how to remain healthy in all kinds of climates and eating different types of food. He also indicated what to do if a passenger became unwell, had a heart attack or even a baby. We were lectured on safety procedures and I learnt how to remove windows and climb out of an aircraft and jump down a chute. We were warned not to wear nylon knickers that day as they could cause a very nasty burn! We went to Hounslow Swimming Baths and each of us was put into a cage which was submerged in the deep end and we had to find the way out and swim to the surface. It was all tremendous fun.

An Elizabeth Arden specialist was brought in to advise us on skincare and makeup and gave each one of us a set in the colour that suited us. We were measured and fitted for our smart uniforms, winter and tropical, we were provided with handbag, hand baggage and suitcase, which just left us to buy our own court shoes!

A large and very important part of our training was the serving of meals. Good food and service sold tickets. At lunch times we left our lecture rooms and sat in a mock-up aircraft and under direction, took it in turns to serve each other lunch, without the drinks of course.

The day eventually arrived, course completed, all exams and tests passed, uniforms fitting, makeup perfectly applied and we were ready for our first flight. I was assigned to the Comet 4 fleet. My first flight was to Singapore with a stopover in Beirut then Karachi.

After the passengers were boarded and seated, hand baggage safely stowed in the racks, we proceeded to demonstrate the use of oxygen masks and lifejackets. I was positioned at the front of the economy class cabin. I was nervous, very nervous, I had never flown before and I accidentally pulled the red tag and my life jacket inflated noisily. I became aware of fifty pairs of surprised eyes staring at me. A few minutes later we took off into the sky and it was wonderful.

I served my apprenticeship in the economy cabin and after about a year I was promoted to first class. In those days the meal service was very formal. The tables were laid with cloths, proper cutlery and glasses and the food was served from a trolley by silver service. On most flights Beluga Caviar was offered with all the accompaniments, the trolley with the main courses, usually beef, was pushed down the cabin and the meat was carved in front of each passenger and a variety of wines offered. I just loved this!

The highlights of my time with BOAC apart from going to utterly amazing places were being selected for royal flights. The first one was from London to San Francisco with Princess Margaret and Lord Snowden shortly after their marriage. I felt enormously proud standing on the gang plank and our captain presenting each one of us to the royals.

The next one was accompanying the Duke of Edinburgh and Princess Anne to Kingston, Jamaica for the Commonwealth Games. We refuelled in New York where we were joined by Prince Charles who had just finished his schooling in Australia. It was only when I returned home that I became aware that there had been some sort of incident and I made the front page of the Peterborough Citizen Advertiser with "Local Girl in Bomb Scare". Our captain obviously did not think it important enough to tell us.

BOAC was a great company to work for. They looked after us so well, we stayed in the best hotels and were given enough money to enable us to eat at good restaurants where ever we were in the world. I started to get seriously interested in food. In London I had a super boyfriend who also took me to lovely restaurants. He bought me Robert Carrier's "Great Dishes of the World" and I started to cook and have dinner parties. He also had a 30-foot boat moored on the Hamble and so I found myself cooking for him and friends on our weekend trips to the Isle of Wight and longer trips to France. Soused herrings were a favourite starter and any sort of casserole that could be reheated. I was more than delighted to do the cooking, I knew nothing of navigation, was rubbish at changing sails, but I could in fact steer a straight course and provide a good lunch.

Having left BOAC to get married, a marriage which sadly only lasted a few months, I got a job with an estate agent. It was during this time that I met Gavin and Nick who were both accountants, both entrepreneurial and were just about to open a Delicatessen in Lacy Road, Putney, a delightful street with a very good butcher and a fish shop which eventually closed down unexpectedly with a notice in the window saying "Gone Fishing". Nick, Gavin and I kept in touch and the day came when they rang to tell me that the property next door to the Deli had become vacant and would I like to fulfil my dream? We put in equal amounts of money and the boys donned their blazers and old school ties and clutching a business plan, went off to see the bank manager to borrow the rest. I handed in my notice and armed with a suitcase full of recipes books and note books flew off to the Gulf of Mexico. I sat on a golden beach, burning my back while I thought up menus and worked out quantities needed for 10, 15 and 20 portions. Back in London the work progressed rapidly headed by Fred the builder. I combed London for second-hand equipment, emptied out my kitchen of appliances, pans, knives, etc. A notice on the shop window and local paper soon brought a variety of individuals so I was able to select my staff.

The night before we opened I was still stitching away at the café curtains, excitement and adrenalin kept me going. Success was almost immediate we were just about full every night. We had only 30 seats and sometimes we did as many as 100 covers. The cooks were girls just out of cookery school and certainly knew a lot more than I did. I learnt so much from them. Many of the recipes in the book originated from them. I think we became popular due to the fun atmosphere, inexpensive menu that was good value for money, together with fresh food cooked daily.

Suzie Moir came to work as front of house during term time when her two children were at school. We had joined BOAC the same day and it was wonderful for me to have my best friend around, she was a huge support. Looking back I was incredibly lucky having such a good team to work with. Being a keen swimmer, I started to go to Putney Swimming Baths and do 30 Olympic lengths before starting work. Before long I was joined by several of the girls. I think it kept us fit and happy.

After a couple of years or so it became obvious that we needed larger premises. It was somewhat of a relief to Nick and Gavin to come to a decision to shut the Deli and expand our restaurant. They had been unlucky in the Deli manager and the slippage that took place. So back on went the old school ties and in came Fred the builder and his team. In no time walls came down and we had a 60 seat restaurant and it was perfectly manageable with the same amount of staff. Financially it was the best thing we could have done.

A few more years passed by and two more properties were acquired and turned into restaurants. By this time I was exhausted. I was working 15 hours a day and not feeling that great. Nick and Gavin were very understanding and found Mark, who was about 25 years younger than I, very well qualified and so I went off to Cape Town for the winter and had a good rest.

On my return I received a phone call from the All England Lawn Tennis Club (AELTC) at Wimbledon inviting me to an interview to take charge of the catering. Wimbledon Fortnight is catered for by a large company, but the rest of the year is very busy with various matches taking place and of course, the members use the courts daily. Running the bar and doing the lunches and teas was quite easy for me. At the interview I was asked whether I was good at making cakes, I had to answer that I had never made a cake but would learn, and the job was mine. Baking cakes was a challenge and I took great pride in giving them a selection of eight different cakes each day. Tea was a popular meal especially at weekends. Lunch was easy because, although there might be a large number to cater for, they were served a set menu. I really enjoyed my time at the AELTC, the Chef Executive, Chris Gorringe and all the staff were delightful and I loved working with them.

I met some really interesting and famous people, Diana Princess of Wales, TV and Radio sports presenters and of course, the tennis players themselves. During the Championships, if ever I had a minute to spare, I would sneak to the back of the Royal Box and watch the match from there. Even when the Championships were over and the crowds gone there was always a tremendous atmosphere on that court. It was not used for any other match throughout the year. It was played on just before the Championships began, by four ladies playing doubles to break it in gently and afterwards, by the Chairman, the Chief Executive and two others, I suppose for the tremendous fun of it. It had been a fascinating time and I was sad to leave, but I am still in touch and get a Christmas card and calendar and am invited to lunch every other year.

My freelancing took me to Enterprise Oil for three months, where my kitchen window looked out onto The Mall and Buckingham Palace. I had several weekends at Sydmonton Court, near Newbury, with Andrew Lloyd Webber. I did directors' lunches and I even did the 'wake' for my dear friend Maureen's husband. This was held in a flat in Putney and while it was going on a nice little man, from the flat immediately below, came up to me and said

BOAC Training Course 1961.
I am second from the left in the front row.

how much he had enjoyed the food and he would very much like me to do his funeral tea and "the whisky is in the cupboard above the sink"!

I had two summers in the Outer Hebrides at Amhuinnsuidhe Castle in Harris, one winter in the Virgin Islands, cooking for Terry Ellis of Chrysalis Records and then I discovered Scotland! I came up for the grouse shooting for Sir Andrew Forbes Leith and after that pheasant shooting at Tulchan Lodge near Grantown-on-Spey. The Lodge had a Christmas party where I met a young and lovely local farmer who had arrived with his mother. The lodge housekeeper, Joan and I became great friends and together we opened the Tea Shop at Ballindalloch Castle where my cake making skills came into use.

It became very clear I could never live in London again so I sold my shares in the restaurants and built a house overlooking the river Spey with Ben Rinnes beyond. I gave up work to look after my mother during her last years and then got back to catering for fishing and shooting parties.

And of course, I married my farmer.

Planning a Menu

Planning a menu will depend on all sorts of things; what ingredients are available, vegetables that are in season, how much you can afford to spend, time available and your own expertise. It is not a good idea to try out a new recipe for a dinner party.

In the following menus there are quite a few dishes that can be prepared in advance and Menu 8 can all be done in advance and even frozen so all you have to do on the day is defrost, reheat the lamb then cook the rice and make the salad. Easy!

On choosing your menu do not be tempted to serve three courses that contain cream as an ingredient or even two, it's a little sickening and also fattening.

Menu 1

Smoked Salmon Tartare with Split Toast

***

*Fillet of Roe Deer
Potatoes Dauphinoise*

***

Ginger & Pear Pudding

Menu 2

Krenzer Salad

***

*Duck Breasts with 5 Spice
New Potatoes*

***

Pavlova Roulade

Menu 3

Beetroot Roulade

***

*Mustard Beef
Mashed Potatoes*

***

Crème Caramel

Menu 4

Stuffed Mushrooms

***

*Pheasant Breasts with Calvados and Ginger
Grilled potato Slices*

***

Chocolate Mousse

Menu 5

Prawns – Chili Garlic

***

Braised Lamb Shanks
Baked Jacket Potato halves

***

Ecclefechan Tart

Menu 6

Pheasant & Pistachio Terrine

***

Creamy Pork & Mushrooms
Rice

***

Banana & Apple Crumble

Menu 7

Prawn & Smoked Salmon Paté

***

Spiced Chicken and Couscous

***

Plum Fudge Puddings

Menu 8

Chicken Liver Paté

***

*Armenian Lamb
Rice and Salad*

***

Iced Grand Marnier Soufflé

Canapés

While I was still involved with Gavin's, I was asked to go to Sydmonton Court near Newbury for a weekend, to cook for Andrew Lloyd-Webber. Fortunately it went well and I was asked back on various occasions, in fact several times, I was invited to work for him full time.

One beautiful October day as I drove through the park to the house, all the gardeners were raking up dead leaves into massive piles. I parked by the kitchen door and started to carry in all my boxes of food. I heard the sound of an aircraft, looked up and saw a helicopter approaching the park. What a sight to see all the leaves go skyward and the helicopter land in the middle of it all. One gardener muttered – "he didn't tell us he was coming by helicopter". With a big smile on his face Andrew climbed out and walked past them all and greeted me.

The house was very lovely and full of incredible pictures – the real thing, but somehow the acoustics were better in the large kitchen where I was trying to work. He would come in with Sarah Brightman, who he was married to at the time, put on a tape and she would sing. He would stop and direct her to what he wanted or would say "more drums here, quieter brass there". It was impossible to work with this amazing 'for real' music going on.

It was a very exciting time. Mr Lloyd-Webber is incredibly talented, not only in music, he likes to cook too. One morning he saw some parsnips that I was going to use with lamb, picked one up and said "let's make parsnip crisps".

So here is the recipe, but don't throw away all the best olive oil as I watched him do!

CHEESE PUFFS

Makes about 80   Heat oven to 200°C/400°F/Gas mark 6

Method

Melt the butter and cheeses
together. Fold the whisked
egg whites into the cheese
mixture, coating well. Using
two forks, dip the bread cubes
into the mixture, coating well.
Lay them on a baking tray
and freeze until solid – probably about 2 hours.

Ingredients

170g (6oz) butter
170g (6oz) mature cheddar cheese
115g (4oz) cream cheese
3 egg whites, whisked
1 large unsliced white loaf cut into
1" cubes (crusts removed)

When frozen they can be bagged up for future use, or if serving
straight away, taken out, placed on a greased baking tray and baked
for 10 minutes until browned and crisp.

PARSNIP CRISPS

Method

Wash, top & tail and peel the parsnips, then using a mandolin, cut strips along the length. It can be done with a vegetable peeler if the parsnips are not too large.

Heat up a wok or saucepan half full of oil and when smoking, drop in a handful at a time of parsnip strips. Remove with a slotted spoon when golden brown and drain on kitchen paper.

Sprinkle with salt and serve.

Ingredients

Parsnips, however many you want
Oil for frying
Salt

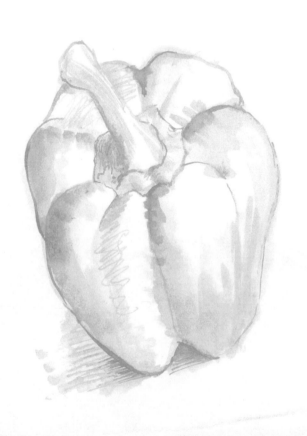

Soups

BROCCOLI and STILTON SOUP

This is a good way to use up any stilton cheese left over from a dinner party. In our restaurant we used to serve half a stilton and allow our customers to help themselves. Because it soon got quite messy, this soup appeared on the menu very regularly.

Serves 4-6

Method

Heat the butter in a large saucepan, add the onion and cook for about 5 minutes until softened. Add the broccoli and stir. Add the stock and simmer until the broccoli is cooked. Crumble in the stilton. Liquidize then season well. Do not add salt until after the addition of the stilton as this cheese is very salty.

Ingredients

25g (1oz) butter
1 large onion chopped
700g (1½lb) broccoli tops,
roughly chopped and stalks finely sliced
850ml (1½pts) chicken or vegetable stock
225gm (8oz) stilton cheese

CELERIAC and LEEK SOUP

Serves 4-6

Method

Heat the butter, add the onions and leeks. Stir around and sauté for a few minutes then add the celeriac and potatoes, again stir around for a few minutes. Add the boiling water, cover and cook until the vegetables are cooked 20-30 minutes. Blend. Add the cream, season and serve hot garnished with chives or parsley.

Ingredients

110g (4oz) butter
1 large onion chopped
450g (1lb) sliced leeks
450g (1lb) celeriac, peeled and sliced
220g (8oz) potatoes, peeled and sliced
2l scant (3pts) boiling water
150ml (5fl oz) double cream
Chopped chives or parsley to garnish

CELERY and GINGER SOUP

Garlic croutons are very good with this, see separate recipe.

Method

Heat the butter and add celery and onion, cooking gently for 2-3 minutes. Add potato and ginger – stir around and cook for another 2-3 minutes. Add stock and a little seasoning. Leave to simmer for 10-15 minutes with the lid on, until the vegetables are cooked. Liquidize, then reheat and add milk and cream

Ingredients

1 head celery, washed and chopped
1 onion, chopped
1 potato, chopped
1" piece root ginger peeled and finely chopped
1 clove garlic, chopped
25g (1oz) butter
570ml (1pt) chicken stock
275ml (½pt) milk
2-3 tablespoons double cream
1 tablespoon parsley, chopped
Salt and pepper

Season, and serve with a sprinkling of parsley.

COURGETTE SOUP

If you have a glut of courgettes this is a good way to use them up, and the soup freezes well.

Method

Heat oil, add onions and cook until soft, add dill seeds and cook for a couple of minutes. Tip in stock and bring up to the boil, add courgettes and simmer for 10-15 minutes. Take off heat, add cream cheese and liquidize. Add seasoning. The result should be a creamy and delicate soup.

Ingredients

700g (1½lb) courgettes, chopped
1 onion, finely chopped
1 teaspoon dill seeds
1.2l (2pts) chicken stock
110g (4oz) cream cheese,
1 tablespoon olive oil

COURGETTE, PEA and PESTO SOUP

It's useful to have a soup that is totally vegetarian.

Serves 6 - 8, or you can halve the quantity for fewer people

Method

Boil water and add the vegetable bouillon. Bring to the boil again and add courgettes, Cook for 5-6 minuets then add the peas and pesto. Taste and add more pesto if preferred. Grind some black pepper but no salt as the stock is already fairly salty.

Ingredients

1kg (2lb 4oz) courgettes, washed and finely chopped
175g (6oz) frozen Peas
2.4l (3½ pts) water
6 teaspoons Marigold Swiss vegetable bouillon
4-5 teaspoons of green pesto

CURRIED PARSNIP SOUP,
Jane Grigson's
There is no better recipe by anyone!

Serves 4-6,

Method

Pulverize above ingredients together and use 1 tablespoon for this recipe. The remainder will keep well in a jar.

Ingredients

1 heaped tablespoon coriander seeds
1 level teaspoon cumin seeds
1 dried red chilli
1 rounded teaspoon ground turmeric
¼ teaspoon ground fenugreek

If you don't have all of the above, 1 tablespoon of curry powder will do just as well

Method

Melt the butter and add a little oil and sauté the onions and garlic for a few minutes. Add the parsnips, spice and flour. Stir round then add the stock. Simmer until the vegetables are soft. Blend, add cream. Reheat adding more water if the soup is too thick. Season and sprinkle over the chives or parsley and serve.

Ingredients

1 medium onion chopped
2 cloves garlic chopped
1 large parsnip peeled and cut up
60g (2oz) butter and a little oil
tablespoon flour
2pts* beef stock (chicken would do)
150ml (¼pt) cream
Chopped chives or parsley
*generous litre

LEEK and POTATO SOUP

Serves 4-6

Method

Melt the butter and add the leeks and onions and cook over a low heat for about 10-15 minutes. Add potatoes and cook for 2-3 minutes then add stock and seasoning. Simmer for 20 minutes until vegetables are soft. Add milk and reheat, add nutmeg and check for seasoning.

Ingredients

3 or 4 leeks, washed and finely sliced
2 med potatoes, peeled and diced
1 large onion, finely chopped
50g (2oz) butter
850ml (1½pts) chicken or vegetable stock
275ml (10fl oz) milk
Chopped chives or parsley for serving
Salt & pepper, small grating of nutmeg

This soup can be served as it is or blended.

MUSHROOM SOUP

Serves 6

Method

Ingredients

Melt half the butter in a saucepan, add the onion and garlic, cover and cook gently for 5 minutes without allowing the mixture to colour. Stir in the flour and cook gently for 1 minute, still stirring. Gradually add the stock, stirring all the time. Add half the

30g (1oz) butter
½ medium onion, finely chopped
1 garlic clove, finely chopped
45g (1½oz) plain flour
625ml (1¼pts) vegetable stock
255g (9oz) chestnut mushrooms, sliced
1 tablespoon finely chopped fresh flat-leaf
    parsley
75ml (3fl oz) single cream
Salt and freshly ground pepper
2 tablespoons flat-leaf parsley, finely chopped

mushrooms and parsley. Cover, bring to the boil and simmer gently for 10-15 minutes, until the vegetables are tender. Cool a little, then liquidize.

In a frying pan melt the remaining butter, sauté the remaining mushrooms until they begin to brown, about 5 minutes, then add to the soup. Simmer gently for 3 minutes. Stir in the cream and taste for seasoning.

Serve garnished with chopped fresh parsley.

RED PEPPER, CARROT and TOMATO SOUP

*Known in my family as **Red Soup***

This is ideal for vegetarians if made with vegetable stock, also for those with gluten allergies as it contains no flour. It freezes really well.

Serves 6

Method

Cut peppers into quarters. Remove pith and seeds, rinse and grill until the skin is blackened. Put into a polythene bag to cool and then the skin will be easier to peel off.

Heat olive oil in a large pan, add cumin seeds and ginger. When the seeds start to pop, add the onions, garlic and carrots. Turn down the heat and cook for about 10 minutes stirring occasionally until onions are transparent. Add peppers and tomato purée, sugar and bay leaves and give it a good stir. Tip in the stock, white wine, salt and pepper and simmer for about 45 minutes or until carrots are soft. Remove the bay leaves and when cool enough blend or liquidize. Rinse out the pan, return the soup and reheat. Before serving add the chopped parsley or coriander.

Serve with warm croutons, crusty French bread or rolls.

Ingredients

450g (1lb) red peppers
450g (1lb) carrots peeled and chopped
1 medium onion finely chopped
2 large cloves of garlic finely chopped
1 rounded teaspoon finely chopped ginger
1 level teaspoon cumin seeds
142g (5oz) tin tomato purée
2 tablespoons olive oil
2 bay leaves
1 rounded teaspoon sugar
1 litre (2pts) good vegetable or chicken stock
250ml (5fl oz) white wine

Seasoning
1-2 tablespoons chopped parsley or fresh coriander to
    garnish

SPICED LENTIL SOUP

This is so good I usually have two helpings!

Serves 4

Method

Heat the oil in the large pan and add the carrot, potatoes and onion. Cook for five minutes then add the chilli, cumin, coriander and turmeric. Cook for two minutes, stir in the lentils and stock, bring to the boil and simmer for 30 minutes until the vegetables and lentils are tender. Add the lemon juice and coriander. Serve in warm bowls and add a spoonful of yoghurt.

Ingredients

1 tablespoon olive oil
1 medium carrot, finely diced
2 potatoes, finely diced
1 medium onion, chopped small
1 dried red chilli, crushed
1 teaspoon ground cumin
2 teaspoons ground coriander
1 teaspoon turmeric
110g(4oz) whole green or brown lentils, washed and drained
1.2l (2pts) vegetable or chicken stock
1 tablespoon fresh lemon juice
1 tablespoon fresh chopped coriander
    Yoghurt

Some Naan bread would be good with this.

THAI TOMATO SOUP

A really delicious soup much loved by my fishing parties who take it in a flask for lunch.

Serves 4-5

Method

Heat butter and soften onions and garlic. Add cumin and ginger. Stir for a couple of minutes. Add tomatoes, vegetable stock and seasoning.

Cook 15-20 minutes, add coconut milk. Taste and add sugar as required to remove acidity of tomatoes. Blend, reheat and serve as it is or sprinkle with parsley or coriander.

Ingredients

2 medium onions, chopped
3 cloves garlic, chopped
½ teaspoon ground ginger
1½ teaspoons of ground cumin
2 tins tomatoes
1l (1¾pts) vegetable stock
1 tin 400ml coconut milk
1 teaspoon sugar
Salt and pepper

Starters

BEETROOT ROULADE
with horseradish Cream

If you like beetroot and horseradish, this is a terrific combination

Serves 5-6   Heat oven to 190°C/375°F/gas mark 5
Line and grease an 8" x 12" Swiss roll tin

Method

Cook the beetroot by steaming or boiling until tender. Peel, and purée in a blender. Beat in the butter, onion and seasoning. Beat in the egg yolks, then whisk the egg whites until stiff and fold into the mixture with a metal spoon. Spoon into the tin and bake for 15 minutes, or until firm and spongy. Turn out onto a sheet of greaseproof paper, carefully peel off the paper in strips and cover with a damp tea towel or muslin till cold.

Ingredients

225g (8oz) raw unpeeled beetroot
25g (1oz) butter
2 teaspoons grated onion
Salt and black pepper
4 eggs, separated

Filling

150ml (¼pt) double cream lightly whipped
2 teaspoons sugar
3 tablespoons chopped parsley
1 tablespoon fresh grated horseradish
or 3 tablespoons horseradish sauce

Combine all the filling ingredients and spread on the base of the roulade. Roll up and chill until required.

Serve with a garnish of beetroot, finely chopped celery and watercress.

CHICKEN LIVER PATE

Method

Fry onion and livers in a third of the butter. Place in food processor with all the other ingredients and another third of the butter. Process until fine then sieve into a terrine, melt the final third of butter and pour over the top to seal.

Ingredients

225g (8oz) chicken livers
175g (6oz) butter divided into three pieces
1 dessertspoon mango chutney
1 small onion
Pinch of ginger
1 tablespoon brandy

CROUTONS

For soup

Ingredients

2-3 slices of white bread, crusts removed (a good way of using up stale bread)

Cut the bread into cubes about 5-10mm (¼ – ½") square. Heat some olive oil in a frying pan and when hot add the bread and fry until golden brown. Drain on kitchen paper and grind over with salt to taste.

For paté and terrines

Heat the oven to 180°C/350°F/gas mark 4
Cut a stick of French bread into diagonal slices about 2½ cm (1") thick. Crush a clove of garlic and mix in a small bowl with 1-2 tablespoonsful olive oil. With a teaspoon spread the oil and garlic on both sides of the cut bread. Place on a baking tray and bake for about 15 minutes or until slightly browned and crisp.

Both types of croutons will last a few days if stored in an airtight container.

HOUMOUS

*Long before **Houmous** became available in our supermarkets, I had a version of this dish one night on a BOAC stopover in Damascus. It was rather runny and served with bread instead of butter. I now think it was Tahinosalata, the same ingredients as Houmous without the chick peas. It became memorable for me because of what happened on the next day. I got up early to go to the Souk where in fact I bought a thin gold bracelet for £5 which to this day I have never taken off. Our hotel was in the main square and as I wandered back there were massive noisy crowds, then to my total horror witnessed a public hanging. One of our crew had also seen this but he had a camera and had photographed it all, the police saw this chased him and searched the hotel but he had hidden his camera in the bathroom water tank .We left that afternoon and I have never been back.*

HOUMOUS

Serves 6

Method

If using the dried chick peas cover them with cold water and cook until soft (about 1 hour) do not add salt at this stage. Drain but keep the liquid. Place all the ingredients in a food processor with about 150ml (5floz) of cooking water or tap water if using tinned and process until smooth. Add more water if too thick. Pour into a bowl, pour on a few drops of olive oil and a dusting of paprika.

Ingredients

225g (8oz) chick peas soaked overnight or
400g (14oz) tin chick peas drained
4 tablespoons tahini (pulped sesame seeds)
2 cloves garlic chopped
75ml (3fl oz) lemon juice
50ml (2fl oz) olive oil
Paprika

Serve with vegetable crudities or fingers of hot pitta bread.

TAHINOSALATA

Serve as a dip

Method

Put all ingredients into a food processor except for the parsley, and process until smooth. Add water to thin it down a bit. Serve in a bowl and sprinkle with parsley.

Ingredients

Half a jar - 150g (5oz) tahini
5 tablespoons lemon juice
2 tablespoons olive oil
2 cloves garlic
Handful of chopped parsley

KIPPER FILLETS, MARINATED

Serves 4-6

Method

Remove skin from the fillets and slice into ¼ inch thick strips. Place into a polythene box, add all the other ingredients and mix well. Leave in cool place for 3-4 days, turning over every now and then.

Ingredients

450g (1lb) boneless kipper fillets
2 small onions finely sliced into rings
½ teaspoon crushed coriander
175ml (6fl oz) Really Good Vinaigrette
Generous amount milled black pepper

After placing the fillets on plates decorate with rocket or green leaves with a wedge of lemon, serve with toast.

KIPPER PATE

Serves 4

Method

In a lidded frying pan cook the fillets in butter until soft. Skin and pulverize in a food mixer. Add the melted butter, the horseradish, Tabasco and Worcestershire sauce and mix in. Whip the cream and fold into the mixture. Season with paprika and black pepper then give it a good stir and spoon into ramekin dishes or a terrine. Cover and refrigerate until needed.

Serve with lemon wedges and toast.

Ingredients

225g (8oz) boneless kipper fillets
15g (½oz) butter
Juice of half a lemon
1 large teaspoon horseradish cream
Tabasco and Worcestershire sauce
250g (8fl.oz) double cream
Paprika and ground black pepper
2 tablespoons melted butter
1 lemon cut into wedges

KRENZER SALAD

My dear friend Maggie gave me this recipe. She went to a farewell dinner in honour of Philippe Krenzer, the Catering Manager at Claridges, who was leaving to start a new job at the Oberoi Hotel in Hong Kong. I think the host put together a wonderful combination of flavours. I wonder what they had for the next course.

Method

Ingredients

Place the eggs in boiling water for 3 minutes. Remove into a bowl of cold water. They are easy to peel while still warm, but return to cold water after peeling until cold. Cut in half lengthwise, carefully remove yolks into a small bowl and mix in a little mayonnaise, a sprinkling of curry powder, a squeeze of lemon juice, some seasoning ,then spoon it back into the whites. Steam or boil the asparagus. On each plate arrange the leaves, the asparagus, the quail eggs and the olives then crumble over the Roquefort and drizzle over the vinaigrette.

Quails eggs - 2 per person
Seasoning, mayonnaise, lemon juice and curry powder
Asparagus, 4-5 spears per person
Black olives, 2-3 per person
Lollo Rosso leaves
Roquefort cheese, about ½oz per person
Seasoning, mayonnaise, lemon juice and curry powder

Serve with good bread for mopping!

In the evenings, most of our clients used to book but for some time a very quiet, nice man used to come in, sometimes with his Chinese wife and sometimes, their daughter as well.

.

One evening, my partner Nick's wife, Carrie was working. During the course of the evening, she said to me that she was sure she recognised the voice of this chap.

I bribed her with a Gin and Tonic to go and ask him.

I watched her walk to his table and saw him smile broadly, obviously thrilled to be recognised – Roy Plomley of Desert Island Discs. After that, he always booked in his name and he became a much-loved client. How sad we all were when he died.

PHEASANT and PISTACHIO
TERRINE with Cumberland jelly

If you are a country dweller and come across creatures killed on the road, this is a good recipe for using up pheasants. You can always make up the weight with chicken breasts. Legally you are not supposed to pick up carcasses if you have hit a bird yourself, it has to be the second vehicle that has the advantage, but I don't think anyone takes much notice these days. Unless you live in the country, you will not come across much game road kill, but happily I was able to get my pheasants from the local gamekeeper when I went home to Northamptonshire. One Sunday evening I drove back to London with a dozen brace of very well hung birds unwrapped on a tray. The smell was so appalling that on arrival I got out of the car and was very sick in the gutter! It took me some time to deal with pheasants again, but I now really enjoy this dish.

PHEASANT and PISTACHIO TERRINE *with Cumberland Jelly*

Serves 6 – 8   Heat oven to 180°C/350°F/gas mark 4
Line a terrine or loaf tin - 900g (2lb) - with foil

Marinade Method

Put all marinade ingredients into a saucepan and simmer for five minutes. Remove from heat and leave to cool completely before pouring over diced raw pheasant. Leave in a cool place overnight. The next day discard the strips of lemon peel from the pheasant marinade.

Marinade Ingredients

4 tablespoons olive oil
150ml (5fl oz) port or red wine
1 onion finely chopped
Thyme – leaves stripped from a
    sprig in your garden
Pared rind of one unwaxed lemon
½ teaspoon salt and plenty
    freshly ground black pepper
2 good pinches mace

Terrine Method

Slit each sausage with the point of a sharp knife and remove the skin. Mix the sausage meat with the pistachios, the pheasant and the marinade (the only way to do this efficiently is with your hands). Lay the bay leaves down the centre of the tin. Run a blunt knife over the rashers of bacon to flatten and lengthen them, then lay them across the tin widthways, their ends overhanging at either side.

Terrine Ingredients

3 bay leaves
8 streaky bacon rashers
    - smoked or unsmoked
675g (1½lb) raw pheasant breasts, diced
450g (1lb) good sausages
55g (2oz) shelled pistachio nuts
2 teaspoons black/brown mustard seeds

56

Pack the mixture into the tin and fold the overhanging bacon on top of the meat. Cover tightly with foil. Put terrine in a roasting tin with water to come half way up the sides of the tin. Cook in oven for two hours. Weight the top (a couple of tins of baked beans does the trick) and leave to cool.

Cumberland Jelly Method

Put ingredients into a saucepan and heat gently until the jelly has dissolved. Pour into warmed jars, cool, seal and keep in the fridge. It is also delicious if you use it before it has set. When the terrine is cold, take off weights and store in the fridge.

Cumberland Jelly Ingredients

250g (9oz) redcurrant jelly
1 tablespoon Dijon mustard
2 teaspoons gelatine powder
150ml (5floz) port
Grated rind and juice of a lemon and an orange

To serve, turn out onto a dish and serve with Cumberland jelly.

PRAWNS, GARLIC and CHILLI

Serves 4

Method

Heat olive oil in large pan then add ginger garlic chillies and prawns, fry and keep on turning it all over until the prawns are cooked, then add the parsley and lemon juice and salt and pepper. Serve with hot French bread or Ciabatta.

Ingredients

16 large raw tiger prawns peeled
2 cloves garlic peeled and finely chopped
1 dessertspoon finely chopped ginger
2-3 medium hot chillies deseeded and
    finely sliced
1 juicy lemon
Handful fresh parsley finely chopped
Olive oil for frying

PRAWN and SMOKED SALMON PATÉ

Serves 4

Method

Put butter, mayonnaise, cream cheese, seasonings and lemon juice in a food processor and mix. Add the prawns, salmon and chopped chives and switch on and off a couple of times or until the prawns are lightly chopped and all mixed in. Using an ice cream scoop or two tablespoons, make rounds of the mixture, place on a tray and refrigerate for an hour until set. Arrange on a plate with mixed leaves to decorate. Serve with a wedge of lemon and some split toast. (See page 62)

Ingredients

225g (8oz) peeled prawns, halved
100g (4oz) smoked salmon, cut into strips
75g (3oz) butter
3 tablespoons mayonnaise
3 tablespoons cream cheese
2 teaspoons lemon juice
Salt and pepper
Pinch cayenne pepper
2 teaspoons chopped chives

SCALLOPS with PEA PUREE and BACON

Serves 4

Method

Melt half the butter in pan, when hot add spring onions and cook until soft. Add peas, sugar and stock, cover and sweat for a few minutes. Add mint and cream and cook until the liquid has evaporated. Season, then liquidise in food processor until smooth. Grill the bacon until crisp.

Ingredients

55g (2oz) butter
6 spring onions, sliced
175g (6oz) frozen peas
1 teaspoon caster sugar
150ml (10fl oz) vegetable stock
2 tablespoons fresh mint leaves chopped
150ml (5fl oz) double cream
4 rashers streaky bacon
3-4 scallops per person

Heat the butter until foaming, add the scallops, and cook for two minutes on either side.

Spoon the purée onto each of the hot plates, then place the scallops in a line on the purée and balance the bacon on the top. A few drops of reduced Balsamic vinegar on the plate looks pretty good too!

SMOKED SALMON TARTARE

This mixture is very versatile and can be incorporated into different canapés, small pastry cases, squares of toast, pitta bread etc.

Serves 4

Method

Place quail's eggs in boiling water for 3 minutes. Turn out into cold water and shell while still warm. With a sharp knife slice salmon into fine strips. Then gently mix in the onion, lemon juice, vodka and some freshly-milled black pepper. Leave for half an hour.

Ingredients

225g (8oz) smoked salmon
1 tablespoon onion – finely chopped
1 teaspoon fresh lemon juice
1 tablespoon vodka
Mayonnaise or soured cream
2 quail's eggs
2 teaspoons capers
Chives, dill or parsley

Divide this into 4 and with the help of a 2½" pastry cutter build a flat castle on each of 4 plates. Add about a teaspoon of mayonnaise or soured cream on the top of each castle then finish off with half a quail's egg, cut side up, and a few capers. Garnish with chives, dill or parsley.

Serve with split toast.

SPLIT TOAST

Method

Toast the bread and with a sharp knife cut off the crusts, then carefully slice through the bread horizontally. Place on baking tray uncooked side up, and put in a medium hot oven until golden brown. These will keep for a day or two in an airtight tin.

Ingredient

1 or 2 slices of bread per person

STUFFED MUSHROOMS

Serves 4   Heat oven to 220°C/425°F/Gas Mark7

Method

Wipe the mushrooms with damp kitchen towel, remove stems, chop, and squeeze out moisture in kitchen paper. Sauté the garlic, onion and mushroom stalks in the oil and half the butter, stir over moderate heat until the liquid has evaporated, about 5 minutes. Mix in remaining ingredients, the parmesan, basil, parsley and seasoning. Stuff the mixture into each mushroom. Top with the remaining butter. Place in a shallow buttered baking dish and place in oven for 15-20 minutes until golden brown.

Ingredients

450g (1lb) large mushrooms
Medium onion finely chopped
1garlic clove finely chopped
40g (1½oz) butter
1tablespoon oil
50g (2oz) grated parmesan
4/5 basil leaves finely chopped
3 tablespoons parsley
Salt and pepper

STUFFED MUSHROOMS, ALMOST INSTANT

In a hurry? Then this is quick and delicious

Heat oven to 220°C/425°F/Gas Mark7

Method

Mix together in a small bowl the cheese and pesto and seasoning. Stuff the mushrooms then dip the tops into breadcrumbs.

Place in shallow buttered baking dish and bake for 15-20 minutes.

Ingredients

3 mushrooms per person, stalks removed
Cream cheese 1 tablespoon per person
Green Pesto, 1 teaspoon per person
Salt and pepper
Breadcrumbs

Garlic bread is delicious with both recipes

SOUSED HERRINGS

This makes an ideal starter and is an excellent source of vitamin D. or try it for a light lunch with potato and green salads. I eat these with great nostalgia, as they bring back such happy memories of sailing weekends.

Serves 3-4   Heat oven to 180°C/350°F/Gas mark 4

Deep, oven proof dish

Method

Have the herrings split and boned and season the inside. Roll up from head to tail and place in a deep dish. Heat together the vinegar and water mixture, the bay leaves, onion and pickling spice. Add salt and bring to the boil, then cool. Pour over the herrings – it should just cover them. Place in oven for about one hour. Serve cold.

Ingredients

6 herring, split and boned
1 tablespoon pickling spice
2 bay leaves
1 red onion, thinly sliced
¾ pt white wine vinegar & water
(in equal proportions)

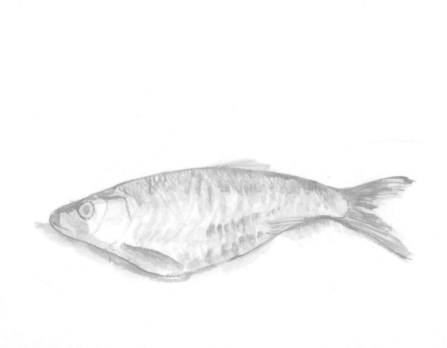

Main Courses

ARMENIAN LAMB

This is a great favourite of mine: happiness is having a box of this tucked away in the freezer!

Heat oven to 180°C/350°F/Gas mark 4

Method

Cut lamb into 1 inch cubes trimming off excess fat. Fry the cubes in hot oil a little at a time and remove to a bowl when well browned and sealed. Then fry the onion slices until soft. Add garlic and after a minute add the spices, stir and finally add the tomato purée, the lentils and the stock or water. Bring to the boil and simmer for one hour, or place in a heated oven.

Serve with rice or couscous and a green salad.

Ingredients

900g (2lb) lamb – boned shoulder
2 onions sliced
2 cloves garlic , crushed
4 tablespoons oil
1 teaspoon ground cumin
½ teaspoon allspice
½ teaspoon turmeric
2 tablespoons brown lentils, washed
  (optional)
2 tablespoons tomato purée
400ml (½ - ¾ pt) stock or water

BEEF SLICES, cooked in white wine and parsley

Serves 4 to 5

Method

Heat a little oil in a heavy frying pan and when smoking add 2-3 slices of beef and brown well on both sides. Remove from the pan and continue to brown the rest. Add a little more oil to the pan if needed, tip in the sliced onions and chopped garlic and stir around until glazed. They will also be browned with the beef sediment. Sprinkle on flour, stir, then gradually add the white wine. Return the beef slices to the pan. Season and add the parsley and thyme, cover and cook on a low heat on or in the oven for about two hours until tender.

This can be served with potatoes, rice or couscous, vegetables or salad.

Ingredients

900g (2lb) braising beef cut up into 1cm slices
2 medium onions, sliced
2 cloves of garlic, chopped
1 dessertspoon flour
½ bottle dry white wine
Salt and pepper
Bunch of parsley, leaves and stalks
2-3 sprigs thyme
Olive oil

BEEF GOULASH

Serves 4-6   **Heat oven 180°C/350°F/Gas mark 4**

Method

Heat oil and brown beef in small amounts then put into a bowl. Fry onions until soft then add paprika, flour, then tomato purée and garlic, stir and pour in stock. When simmering, add the beef, season, cover and simmer on top of oven or inside for about 2 hours or until the meat is tender. Add peppers and tomatoes and simmer for a few more minutes. Spoon cream or yoghurt over the top and serve with potatoes or noodles.

Ingredients

900g (2lbs) chuck steak cut into 1" cubes
2 large onions, sliced
2 tablespoons oil
1 tablespoon paprika
1 tablespoon flour
2 tablespoons tomato purée
2 cloves garlic, crushed
350ml (12fl oz) stock or water
1 red pepper cut into strips and
    blanched
2-3 tomatoes skinned and chopped
150ml (5oz) sour cream or yoghurt

A green vegetable or salad would add good colour

BEEF STIR FRY

I buy tail ends of fillet which are a lot cheaper and make me feel less extravagant! I frequently make this quick and delicious supper.

Serves 2-3

Method

Place steak in a bowl with the cornflour, Chinese five-spice and soy sauce. Mix well and leave to marinate for 20 minutes. Split the broccoli into florets. Slice the stalks diagonally into thin oval shapes and the florets into small heads.

Heat the oil in a wok or large frying pan, add the marinated steak, ginger

Ingredients

375g (12oz) rump, sirloin or fillet steak cut into very thin strips
1½ level tablespoons cornflour
¼ teaspoon Chinese Five Spice
3 tablespoons light or dark soy sauce
175g (6oz) broccoli
2 tablespoons sesame or olive oil
1 tablespoon chopped fresh ginger
1 clove garlic, finely chopped
1 red pepper thinly sliced
1 bunch spring onions sliced diagonally
4-5 tablespoons sherry
2 tablespoons water

and garlic and stir fry for 3-4 minutes. Add the pepper, broccoli and onions then fry again for 2 minutes. Add the sherry and water, put a lid on the pan and steam for one minute. Transfer to a warmed serving dish and serve immediately with noodles or rice.

A few cashew nuts can be added at the last minute for extra crunch.

BOBOTIE

This is a Malay dish which I was given while in Cape Town. It is now a favourite. It can be made using minced beef, but I do think minced lamb is better. If there are any leftovers, they are good cold with salad.

Serves 4   Heat oven to 190°C/375°F/Gas mark 5

Method

Heat a large frying pan until really hot, add the lamb and stir around until brown and crumbly, remove. In the same pan add the oil and when hot add the onion and garlic and when softened, add the spices and bay leaf. Stir for a minute and return the cooked mince. Then add the wine, vinegar and brown sugar, cover and simmer for 10 minutes. Lastly, add the breadcrumbs, almonds and chutney, season well and pour into serving dish.

Ingredients

450g (1lb) minced lamb
1 large onion, peeled and chopped
2 cloves garlic, peeled and crushed
1 tablespoon oil
1 level teaspoon each of mustard seeds, turmeric and garam masala
1 bay leaf
1 tablespoon curry powder
60ml (2½fl oz) each of white wine and white wine vinegar
1 tablespoon brown sugar
1 tablespoon soft white bread crumbs
2 large tablespoons flaked almonds
2 tablespoons mango chutney
Salt and pepper

Topping

250ml (8fl oz) milk
1 large egg, beaten

73

Top with the combined egg and milk. Place the dish on a baking sheet and into the oven for 20 minutes or until the topping is brown.

Serve with rice and a mixed leaf salad.

BRAISED LAMB SHANKS
with flageolet beans

Serves 4   Heat oven to 150°C/300°F/gas mark 2

Method

Dust the lamb shanks with flour and seasoning and brown gently in hot oil in a casserole dish. Remove to a plate and add onions and garlic to oil and sauté until soft. Add mixed herbs, harissa, tomato purée and red wine, then return the browned shanks to the pan. Bring to the boil and cook slowly in oven for 2½ hours until the meat is almost falling off the bone. Drain the flageolet beans and tip into the casserole. Reheat, and serve with rice

Ingredients

4 lamb shanks
2 large onions, chopped
4 cloves garlic, chopped
Olive oil
1 teaspoon mixed herbs
2 teaspoons harissa paste
2 tablespoons tomato purée
225ml (½pt) red wine
1 tin, 410g, flageolet beans

CHILLI CON CARNE

*This was one of the most popular dishes served at
Gavin's – a really good lunch time special. We used to
write the specials on a blackboard and put it on the pave-
ment. One Saturday it brought in Tom Courtney. We
were buzzing that day and he took the last and worst table, the one near the door where you got your elbows
bumped. He was very smiley and charming, however, he
never returned, such a shame as he was a close neighbour,
our gardens backed on to each other. I had much admira-
tion for him since seeing him in 'The Dresser' with Albert
Finney.*

*Another famous neighbour was Felicity Kendall, who
lived opposite me. She always said a cheerful 'good morning', but never came over our threshold.*

CHILLI CON CARNE

Serves 4-5

Method

Heat the oil in a small pan, stir in the onions and then cover with dampened, greaseproof paper and a lid. Leave on a low heat for 10 to 15 minutes. Meanwhile, heat up a frying pan and when hot add beef mince, the beef will have sufficient fat in it. Stir around and break up any lumps, fry until it is browned, add the garlic and all the spices, using less of the chilli if you prefer a mild taste and stir for a minute, then add the tomatoes and the stock, the sugar and seasoning. Cover and simmer on a low heat. Half way through add the drained kidney beans.

Serve this with plain white basmati rice and a green salad.

Ingredients

1 large onion, chopped
2 large cloves of garlic, crushed
1 tablespoon oil
500g (1lb 2oz) beef mince
1-2 teaspoons mild chilli powder
½ teaspoon ground cinnamon
1 teaspoon dried oregano
1 teaspoon paprika
275ml (½pt) stock
2 400g (14oz) cans tomatoes
1 400g (14oz) can red kidney beans
1 teaspoon sugar
Seasoning

CREAMY PORK and MUSHROOMS

Serves 6   Heat oven to 180°C/350°F/Gas mark 4

Method

In a frying pan, heat the butter until sizzling and brown the chops or loin slices on both sides.

Season on both sides with salt, pepper and thyme. Line a flat baking dish with kitchen foil and arrange the pork on it. In the same pan fry the garlic and mushrooms, add the wine and lemon juice simmer for a minute then sprinkle over the flour and mix well. Spoon this over the pork portions and then spoon over the cream. Seal tightly in the foil so none of the juices can escape. Bake in the oven for 40 minutes.

Serve with boiled new potatoes, a green vegetable or salad or all three!

Ingredients

6 large pork chops or 1 inch thick loin slices. Trim off fat
50g (2oz) butter
2 teaspoons fresh thyme chopped or 1teaspoon dried thyme
350g (12oz) mushrooms sliced
2 cloves of garlic crushed
Juice of 1 large lemon
3 tablespoons white wine or water
1 large tablespoon plain flour
150ml (5fl oz) double cream
Salt and pepper

Whenever I cook Duck Breasts I think of an elderly couple who used to come to our restaurant once a week, usually for Sunday lunch. Mabel, what a character, was the cloakroom attendant at Annabel's and Bill was retired and a devoted husband. Sometimes they were accompanied by other members of Annabel's staff, waiters, the door keeper and Mabel's relief help. They were an extremely jolly and appreciative crowd and I became very fond of them. However many of them were there the bill would always be paid with handfuls of silver change counted out in little pieces. I always said how pleased I was to get change!

I was lucky enough to be taken to Annabel's now and then and we got fantastic treatment. The doorman parked our car and we had attentive staff hovering over us. Of course, we got first-hand information on what Lady Diana Spencer was wearing and who were her companions.

Duck à L'orange was Mabel's favourite and I remember one busy night it was served covered with pork gravy instead of orange sauce. No complaints, much laughter! I have left that recipe behind me because I think there are so many better ways to do it and this is one of the best ones.

DUCK BREASTS
with five-spice, honey, soy sauce and lemon

Serves 4   Heat oven to 180°C/350°F/Gas mark 4

Method

Ingredients

Rub the five-spice powder onto both sides of the duck breasts. Heat up a heavy bottomed oven-proof frying pan and when hot add the breasts, skin side down. No fat is needed as duck is a fatty meat and will produce its own.

4 small duck breasts
4 teaspoons five-spice powder
Salt & pepper
2 tablespoons clear honey
2 tablespoons lemon juice
4 tablespoons soy sauce

Cook 3-4 minutes until the skin is a golden brown and then turn over and give this side 3-4 minutes depending how pink you like it. Remove and allow it to rest for 5 minutes. Put the honey, lemon juice and soy sauce into a pan and stir and heat. Slice the breasts onto a serving plate and pour over the sauce.

These are good served with rice or noodles or potatoes.

JILLY'S FISH PIE

Soon after we opened the doors of Gavin's we were honoured and delighted to have Jilly Cooper as a frequent guest. She came in at least once a week for lunch or dinner. The lunches were usually business and evenings, social with her husband, Leo. They were always delightful and charming, interested in what was new – whether it be food, chefs or waiting staff.

Jilly so very kindly chose us as her favourite when well-known people were interviewed about their favourite restaurant. I still have a recording of the Capital Radio interview. During this period my mother came to stay with me while she was having cancer treatment at a London hospital and she usually walked down the road to Gavin's for supper. I remember Leo once leaving the party he was with to sit with her for half an hour.

If there was fish pie on the menu, Jilly usually chose it. Whenever she had a party I did the catering and amongst other things there was always fish pie.

JILLY'S FISH PIE

Serves 4   Heat oven to 180°C/375°F/Gas mark 5

Method

Place the fish in a roasting tin, skin side up. Heat the milk with the onion, peppercorns, bay leaf and salt and pour over the fish. Cover with greaseproof paper, cook for 15 minutes. Strain off the milk and reserve for the sauce. Remove all skin and bones and flake the fish into a large bowl. Add eggs, prawns, capers and parsley then seasoning.

In a saucepan melt the butter, add the flour, beat well and add the reserved milk a little at a time, while beating hard. When the sauce has thickened and all the milk used, pour into the bowl with the other ingredients and carefully mix together, taste and season. Scrape the mixture into an ovenproof dish and when cooled and set slightly, fork the mashed potatoes onto the pie.

Ingredients

900g (2lb) haddock, cod or whiting
    – ½ fresh ½ smoked
425ml (¾pt) milk
½ onion, sliced
8 black peppercorns
1 bay leaf
Salt and pepper
2 hard-boiled eggs, roughly chopped
100g (4oz) prawns
½ tablespoon capers, roughly chopped
Seasoning
1 tablespoon parsley, chopped

For the Sauce

40g (1½oz) butter
25g (1oz) flour
Reserved milk

Topping

675g (1½lb) mashed potatoes

Place in oven for about 20 minutes or until the top is browned.

MEATBALLS
With Tomato & Pepper Sauce

Serves 8-10

Method, Meatballs

Mix all the meatball ingredients together and with both hands roll them into balls (heaped dessertspoon), then roll in the seasoned flour. Fry in hot oil a few at a time until well browned. Keep warm. This should make 40 meatballs.

Method, Sauce

In the same pan fry onions until soft, blend in the flour and add remaining ingredients. Stir, bring to simmering point and add meat balls. Cover and simmer for an hour.

Serve with any pasta, rice, couscous or potato.

Ingredients, Meatballs

450g (1lb) minced beef
450g (1lb) minced pork
75g (3oz) breadcrumbs
50g (2oz) grated parmesan
1 tablespoon parsley
2 teaspoons seed mustard
2 teaspoons horseradish sauce
2 crushed cloves garlic
2 eggs, beaten
¼ pt milk
Seasoned flour for rolling
Oil for frying

Ingredients, Sauce

2 large onions, chopped
1 tablespoon plain flour
2 14oz can tinned tomatoes
2 green peppers, cored, seeded and sliced
Salt and pepper
Worcestershire sauce
1 teaspoon sugar
1 bay leaf

MUSTARD BEEF

I cook this dish using beer. You could use red or white wine or even good stock, but I do think that beer is best!

Serves 4-6   Heat oven to 140°C/275°F/Gas mark 1

Method

Heat the oil in a large flame proof casserole and when very hot, sear the meat, a few pieces at a time, turn them around until well sealed and a rich dark brown. Remove to a plate. When complete, add the onions and stir them around until brown round the edges.

Return the meat and juices to the pan and sprinkle over the flour, stir then gradually add the beer and bring to simmering point. Add the mustard, thyme, bay leaves, garlic and seasoning and stir well.

Ingredients

900g (2lb) chuck or round steak
    cut into 1-2 inch squares
1 tablespoon oil
2 medium onions cut in half and
    each half into 4
1 tablespoon flour
425ml (15fl.oz) Lager or light ale
(or a can with a sip out of it)
2 Sprigs fresh thyme or
levelled teaspoon of dried thyme
2 bay leaves
2 large cloves of garlic, crushed
2 heaped tablespoons of whole
    grain mustard
Seasoning

Cover with a tight fitting lid and place in oven for 2½ hours. Mashed potatoes are good with this, also green or red cabbage or whatever is in season.

PEPPERED FILLET of ROE DEER

Method

Add some olive oil onto a plate and turn the fillets in the oil.

Sprinkle black pepper on all sides of the fillet and leave for ½ to 1 hour. Heat a frying pan (preferably ridged) without adding oil, until very hot. Put in the fillets and cook on each side for 3 minutes, the fillets will be pink on the inside, leave for longer if you prefer. Set aside for 5 minutes.

To serve, slice diagonally and plate up. As there is minimal fat in venison it would be good to serve sauté potatoes and a mixed leaf salad.

Sour cream with a few capers mixed in also goes well with this.

Ingredients

175g (6oz) fillet per person
Black pepper, coarse ground
Olive oil
Salt

PHEASANT BREASTS
With Calvados & Ginger

This is an excellent way of using up road kill when the bird might be a bit damaged – cheap too!

Serves 4   Heat oven to 190°C/375°F/Gas mark 5

Method

Season the breasts. Heat the butter in an oven proof pan and sear the breasts, skin side down until golden, turn over and place pan in oven for 8 to 10 minutes, for pink inside.

Ingredients

4 pheasant breasts, bones removed
1 tablespoon butter
½ onion, finely chopped
2 tablespoons Calvados (brandy will do)
1 teaspoon lemon juice
1 piece stem ginger, finely chopped
1 dessertspoon ginger syrup
75ml (2½fl oz) game or chicken stock
75ml (2½fl oz) double cream

To make the sauce, heat together the Calvados, ginger and ginger syrup, onion, stock and lemon juice and simmer for 4 to 5 minutes. Add cream and season then simmer for another minute.

To serve, slice each breast into 4 to 5 pieces, arrange on a plate and drizzle over with the sauce.

PORK and MUSHROOMS in CIDER

Serves 6-8   Heat the oven to 140°C/275°F/Gas mark 1

Method

Ingredients

Heat some oil in a large flame proof casserole, then add the pork in small batches and fry until brown. Remove to a plate and keep warm. Add the onions and garlic to the pan and cook until brown, then sprinkle over the flour and sage and stir around. Add the pork to the onions then the cider and soy sauce and seasoning. Give it all a good stir and place in the oven (or bottom oven of Aga) and leave for 1½ hours. Remove to add the mushrooms, then return to the oven for another half hour or until the pork is cooked.

1.3kg (3lb) shoulder of pork, fat removed and cut into bite size pieces
3 large onions, sliced
4 cloves garlic, finely chopped
2 large teaspoons dried sage
1 tablespoon plain flour
275ml (½pt) dry cider
2 tablespoons soy sauce
Seasoning
450g (1lb) mushrooms thickly sliced

Good with potatoes boiled, baked or mashed and with any vegetables or salad.

SPICED CHICKEN and COUSCOUS

Serves 2   Heat oven to 200°C/ 425°F/Gas mark 7

Method

Ingredients

350g (12oz) Chicken breasts
½ teaspoon crushed chilli
¼ teaspoon cinnamon
2 tablespoons oil
4 garlic cloves crushed
3 teaspoons curry powder
125g (4oz) couscous
50g (2oz) butter
Salt and black pepper to taste

Cut chicken into bite size pieces and place into a shallow oven proof dish. Mix the oil, garlic and spices together in a small bowl, add a little salt then stir into the chicken. Leave for 20 minutes. Grease with butter another shallow oven proof dish add the couscous, season well, then pour over 200g (8oz) water and top it with slivers of butter. Cover with foil.

Place the chicken in the oven for 20 minutes, after 5 minutes put in the couscous. Remove from the oven and add slivers of butter to the couscous. Fork it over to break up lumps.

Serve with a bowl of yoghurt which is especially good if the chillies are hot. Also a green or mixed or just tomato salad goes well.

STICKY CHICKEN THIGHS
with mustard, lemon and honey

Serves 3   Heat oven to 200°C/400°F/Gas mark 6

Method

Put the peppercorns, lemon juice, honey, mustard and garlic into a bowl and mix well. Trim the fat and underneath skin of the thighs and place in a shallow ovenproof dish skin side down. Spoon the contents of the bowl over the chicken and leave to marinate for half an hour or longer. Sprinkle with salt and place in oven for 20 minutes. Remove and turn the thighs over, now skin side up. Return to oven for a further 20-25 minutes or until the skin is a dark golden brown.

Ingredients

6 Large chicken thighs, bone in skin on
1 Rounded teaspoon crushed
    peppercorns
5-6 tablespoons lemon juice
2 tablespoons runny honey
1 dessertspoon grain mustard
2 garlic cloves crushed
Salt to taste

Serve with rice, couscous, or potatoes and a fresh green salad dressed of course with the Really Good Vinaigrette.

TOAD in the HOLE
With Onion Gravy

Serves 4   Heat oven to 220°C/425°F/Gas mark 7

unless you have a husband like John, who can eat most of it.

Method

To make the batter, sift the flour and salt into a bowl, make a well and break the eggs into it. Whisk together adding a little milk. It will be very thick at this stage add more milk and beat well, incorporating air that will make the pudding rise. Then lightly whisk in the remaining milk and leave to stand for 15 minutes.

Ingredients

450g (1lb) best pork sausages
110g (4oz) flour
2 eggs
300ml (½pint) liquid using ¾
    milk and ¼ water
Salt
Dripping

Meanwhile, partially cook the sausages either by frying or grilling until just coloured. Heat a little dripping in a roasting pan on top of the stove. Add the sausages and pour in the batter. Transfer to the hot oven and bake for 35 to 45 minutes until the batter has risen and the sausages are brown.

While this is cooking make the gravy (see page 91).

ONION GRAVY

Method

Heat some butter in a saucepan and add onions and carefully cook until soft and transparent. Mix in the flour and then gradually add the stock until it reaches a consistency of covering the back of a spoon. A few drops of gravy browning can be added to give a good colour.

Ingredients

1 large onion, peeled halved and thinly sliced
25g (1oz) flour
150ml (½ pint) chicken or vegetable stock
Seasoning

Serve with the **Toad in the Hole**. A little mashed potato and some lightly shredded cabbage is good with this.

VENISON CASSEROLE

This dish is fairly time consuming but it does serve about 8. If you are cooking it for 4 it's worth putting the rest in the freezer. Happiness is, knowing that you have a good meal in the freezer for when you are tired, in a hurry or have unexpected guests.

Low oven temperature 140°C/275°F/Gas mark 4

Method

Mix the marinade ingredients together and pour over the diced venison. Cover and leave for 24 hours. Fry the bacon in a large casserole until the fat runs, take out and place to one side. Fry the onions until softened take out and place to one side.

Drain the meat from the marinade, keeping the marinade for later.

Marinade Ingredients

4 tablespoons olive oil
300ml (½pt) red wine
2 cloves garlic, crushed
½ teaspoon mace
1 slice lemon
2 bay leaves
1 teaspoon coarse ground pepper
6 crushed juniper berries
2 tablespoons red wine vinegar

Method

Dry off the venison pieces and fry in small batches, adding a little oil as necessary. Return all the venison, bacon and onion to the casserole. Sprinkle over the flour and mix in, add the marinade and when thickened, pour in the stock/wine mixture then add the mushrooms, rosemary tomato purée and the chosen jelly.

Cover and cook in a low oven for 2 to 3 hours, depending on the venison.

Casserole Ingredients

1.8kg (4lb) diced venison
350g (12oz) smoked streaky bacon, diced
2 onions, peeled and sliced
1½ tablespoons flour
350g (12oz) mushrooms, sliced
2 or 3 sprigs of rosemary, leaves removed and finely chopped
450ml (¾pt) red wine and stock mixed
(chicken, vegetable or even lamb)
1 dessertspoon tomato purée
2 tablespoons redcurrant, rowan or cranberry jelly

Potatoes

BAKED JACKET POTATO HALVES

Method

Cut the potatoes in half lengthways. With a sharp knife cut each one in a criss-cross pattern with shallow cuts. Dry the tops with a paper towel and rub over with olive oil.

Ingredients

1 medium potato per person
Olive oil
Seasoning

Dust with a seasoning of salt and pepper, Season-all, cumin or even curry powder.

Place on a baking tray and cook until the tops are golden.

A hot or medium oven is fine, whatever the oven is set for if you are cooking something else.

CRISPY POTATO CAKES

These potato cakes are quick and easy to make and they can accompany omelettes, fish, meat or are delicious on their own or with salad.

Method

Grate the potatoes into a bowl of cold water to extract the starch. Drain and place in a clean, dry tea towel and squeeze out as much water as possible.

Ingredients

1 kg (2.2 lbs) potatoes, peeled
2 eggs
2/3 spring onions, finely sliced
Seasoning
Olive oil for frying

Beat the eggs in a bowl and mix in the potato, onion and seasoning. In a large frying pan, heat the oil and when smoking, add handfuls of the potato mixture and flatten slightly, brown on both sides.

GRILLED COOKED, SLICED POTATOES

For this you will need a ridged frying pan

Method

Spoon a little oil over the potatoes ensuring that each slice is oiled on both sides.

Heat up the pan

Ingredients

Any cooked potatoes, sliced
Failing that, use raw potatoes, peeled and cut
    into 1cm (¼") slices then cooked in boiling,
    salted water until just tender
Oil for coating
Salt for serving

until really hot and cook the oiled potato slices on both sides until well marked. Sprinkle with salt and serve hot.

JACKET POTATOES

These potatoes are so versatile. They can be served on their own, they can have different toppings or they can be stuffed by cutting in half lengthways and the contents mixed with a filling, replaced and re-heated.

Heat oven to 190°C/375°F/Gas mark 5

Method

To prepare, wash and dry each potato and then oil and salt the skin, this gives a crisp and well coloured result. Either prick the skin or make a cut in the top, this prevents the potato bursting. Depending on the size they will take 1-1½ hours in a medium hot oven.

Topping suggestions

Garlic butter, grated cheddar or similar, green or red pesto, cream cheese mixed with green or red pesto, herby cream cheese such as Roule or simply sour cream and chives.

Stuffing suggestions

Sliced leeks cooked in butter, grated cheese, cream cheese, green pesto.

After mixing the potato and stuffing of choice, replace into the skins, top with grated cheese and this will result (if placed in the top of the oven) with a delicious melting finish.

POTATO and CABBAGE CAKES

These are good for using up mashed potato and shredded cabbage but it is well worth cooking some of each to make these cakes.

Method

Mix together equal quantities of potato and cabbage. Season well. Transfer to a plate, flatten and cut into wedges. Take up each wedge with your hands, make a round, flat cake. Dust both sides with flour.

Heat oil in frying pan and when hot, fry each potato cake on both sides until golden brown.

These are delicious served with cold meat or grilled bacon or on their own with salad.

POTATOES BOULANGERE

Serves 4-6   Heat oven to 180°C/350°F/gas mark 4

Shallow, flame-proof gratin dish - buttered

Method

Ingredients

Layer the potatoes and onions into the dish, seasoning as you go and make sure there is a neat overlapping of potato slices on the top. Dot the

900g (2lb) potatoes
- King Edward or Maris Piper
1 medium onion, thinly sliced
300ml (½pt) chicken or vegetable stock
25g (1oz) butter
Salt and pepper

top with the remaining butter and pour over the stock. By pressing down the potatoes with a fork, they should be covered with the stock. Bake for 1½ - 2 hours, or until the top is golden brown and the potatoes are tender.

POTATOES DAUPHINOISE

Serves 6-8   Heat oven to 150°C/300°F/Gas mark 2

Method

Ingredients

Peel and slice the
potatoes as thinly
as possible. Heat
the milk and
cream together
with the garlic,
salt and pepper

1kg (2½lb) potatoes. King Edward or Maris Piper
3 cloves garlic
2 teaspoons salt – white pepper
300ml (½pt) double cream
300ml (½pt) milk
50g grated parmesan (optional)

then add the sliced potatoes, making sure that each slice is covered
with the liquid. Bring to the boil then simmer gently until the potato
is tender and the mixture has thickened.

Transfer carefully, without breaking the potato, into a buttered oven-
proof dish. Smooth and sprinkle over the grated parmesan (if using).
Bake for about 1 hour, or until the top is golden brown. This dish
can be made, cooled and re-heated when needed. For a 'posh' presen-
tation allow it to get cold then, using a 3 inch scone cutter, cut out
rounds and place on a greased baking dish and reheat when
required.

Salads

The wash-hand basin and the lettuce!

In the first few weeks of opening Gavins we were regularly visited by a member of the health and safety department. In fact, we were unable to get a license for alcohol until we fulfilled all their demands which included a cover over the passage to the gent's outside W.C. and the necessity for the kitchen staff to have a wash-hand basin. It was not enough that we had a double sink and plenty of paper towels. Money was really tight at this stage but dear Kenny Moir, Suzie's husband, came to our rescue. He plumbed in a tiny little basin under a shelf and all was well. Actually, it was not. Mr Health & Safety dropped in on us one morning to find a lettuce refreshing itself in our little hand basin. Harsh words were exchanged. However, Mr Health & Safety was not all bad, he called in one lunch time to find us having champagne as it was my birthday. By coincidence, it was his birthday too and so every year afterwards he would drop in for a glass and we had little trouble thereafter.

BEETROOT
with Horseradish, Yoghurt and Mint

For a passionate lover of beetroot these recipes are a great improvement on the usual sliced beetroot covered in malt vinegar. The first one is excellent as a dip and wonderful with cold roast beef and perfect with barbecued sausages, beef steaks, venison steaks and burgers.

Heat oven to 180°C/350°F/Gas mark 4

Method

Wash the beetroot, trim and leave on 2-3 inches of stalk to prevent bleeding. Wrap in foil and bake in oven until tender. Small beets will take 1 hour and large ones about 2 hours. Cool and peel.

Ingredients

225g (8oz) raw beetroot
2 tablespoons horseradish sauce
75ml (3fl oz) plain yoghurt
1 dessertspoon chopped mint
Seasoning

Place in a food processor with the yoghurt and horseradish and pulverize briefly. The result you are aiming for is a coarse purée.

BEETROOT, RAW

Peel and coarsely grate the beetroot.

Add seasoning and mix with vinaigrette with some added mustard.

BEETROOT with WHITE WINE VINEGAR

Using cooked beetroot – slice beetroot into a serving dish, leave small beets whole and sprinkle all over some white wine vinegar

CARROT and WALNUT SALAD

A great combination

Serves 4

Method

Mix the ground cumin into the vinaigrette. Add all the other ingredients and mix well.

Ingredients

4 large carrots peeled and grated
3 tablespoons vinaigrette
¼ teaspoon ground cumin
1 tablespoon chopped mint
40g (1½oz) walnuts roughly chopped
Seasoning of salt and pepper

CHICORY and WATERCRESS SALAD

Ingredients

2 heads of chicory sliced
½ bag of washed watercress

CELERIAC REMOULADE

This salad is utterly delicious. With its mustard flavour it is particularly good with any cold meat, also smoked fish. It keeps well for several days if covered and kept in a fridge. Use home-made mayonnaise if you have it, but bought will do very well.

Serves 4 to 6

Method

Ingredients

Peel and cut the celeriac info fine matchsticks. Blanch in boiling, salted water for a minute. Drain and refresh in cold water. Put into a bowl with the lemon juice and turn it over to coat the celeriac. This will retain a good

1 small celeriac – about 450gms (1 lb)
Juice of 1 lemon
4 tablespoons mayonnaise
1 tablespoon Dijon mustard
1 tablespoon capers roughly chopped
2 teaspoons finely chopped gherkin
2 teaspoons finely chopped tarragon
2 teaspoons finely chopped parsley

colour. Put the parsley to one side and mix all the other ingredients together. Stir in the celeriac then transfer to a serving dish.

Sprinkle the parsley over.

NEW POTATO SALAD

Summer salads with barbecues or cold fish or meats can be delicious, especially if you want to avoid too much mayonnaise.

Serves 4

Method

Boil the potatoes in salted water until tender. This should take 8-10 minutes. Drain and leave in colander until the heat of the potatoes has dried off the wetness, then place in serving bowl and pour over 4 to 5 tablespoons of vinaigrette while still warm and gently spoon over until each potato has absorbed the dressing.

Ingredients

1 kg (2lbs) new or waxy potatoes cut into bite-sized pieces
3 dessertspoons capers roughly chopped
2 dessertspoons gherkins chopped
A bunch of spring onions sliced finely
A handful each of parsley, chives and dill, all finely chopped
3 hard boiled eggs
Vinaigrette

When cool, season and add the capers, gherkins, onions and the chopped herbs. The eggs should be placed into boiling water for 7 minutes then tipped into cold water until cool enough to handle, then peel, quarter and add to the salad.

PANZANELLA

I first had this salad on a walking holiday in Tuscany. After we had walked about 10 long miles this was brought out to us together with a variety of salami and chilled Tuscan white wine – it was worth the pain. The Tuscans devised this recipe to use up their stale bread, but I buy it to use the next day.

Serves 4 - 6

Method

Char the peppers over a gas flame or place under a grill until they have blistered and blackened. Place in a covered bowl to cool. This helps to remove the skins. Take out the white bit and seeds, slice. Whisk together the oil, vinegar, salt and fresh ground black pepper then add all the vegetables, herbs and garlic. Tear the bread into bite-sized pieces. If the bread is very stale, moisten with water and then fold in with the vegetables.

Ingredients

1 Ciabatta loaf – 1-2 days old
450g (1lb) tomatoes, deseeded and chopped
1 red and 1 yellow pepper
1 cucumber, peeled, deseeded and chopped
1 or 2 garlic cloves, finely chopped
1 tablespoon capers
6 spring onions, chopped
6 tablespoons olive oil
2 tablespoons red wine vinegar

The amount of oil and vinegar may vary depending on how much bread is used. Refrigerate for a couple of hours before serving.

Sauces

MAYONNAISE

Method

Place the eggs in processor or liquidiser together with the garlic, mustard, salt and pepper and lemon juice. Turn on and pour in the oil slowly, the result should be fairly thick. Lastly add the vinegar.

Ingredients

2 eggs
1 clove garlic, crushed
1 teaspoon mustard powder
1 level teaspoon salt
Black or white pepper
300ml (½pint) olive oil
½ tablespoon lemon juice
1 tablespoon white wine vinegar

Adding the vinegar at the end makes it less likely for the mayonnaise to curdle. Taste for seasoning.

AIOLI SAUCE

As above, but use 4 to 5 garlic cloves

TARTARE SAUCE

Use about 1 heaped tablespoon of mayonnaise per person. To this add some chopped gherkins, capers and parsley.

REALLY GOOD VINAIGRETTE

Couldn't be better for avocado vinaigrette!

Method

Place all the ingredients in a mixing jug and blitz them for about 10 seconds.

Store in jar or bottle until needed, this will keep for some weeks.

Ingredients

1 tablespoon Dijon mustard
100ml (3½oz) white wine vinegar
100ml (3½oz) balsamic vinegar
200ml (7oz) hazelnut oil
200ml (7oz) sunflower oil
200ml (7oz) olive oil
1 teaspoon salt
¼ teaspoon white pepper
1 clove garlic crushed

VINAIGRETTE - DIET OPTION

This is a good way to cut down on the calories, but the better the balsamic vinegar the better the taste will be.

Method

Put all ingredients into a jar and mix or shake thoroughly.

Ingredients

1 tablespoon Dijon mustard
5 tablespoon balsamic vinegar
1 teaspoon oil
1 clove garlic, crushed or left whole
8-10 fresh basil leaves, chopped
Salt and black pepper

Puddings
&
Desserts

AMARETTO ALMOND CAKE

The final soaking of the cake with almond liqueur makes this a particularly delicious recipe. Eat it as it is, or for a pudding with a dollop of crème fraîche and perhaps some poached rhubarb.

Heat oven to 150°C/300°F/Gas mark 2
2lb loaf tin, greased and lined

Method

Cream the sugar and butter until light and fluffy. Beat in the eggs and almonds and then fold in the flour. Scrape into the prepared loaf tin. Bake for 35-40 minutes until golden brown and springy to the touch. Make holes with a skewer and spoon the amaretto over the cake.

Leave to cool before removing from the tin

Ingredients

170g (6oz) caster sugar
170g (6oz) butter
3 eggs
85g (3oz) ground almonds
        (freshly ground, if possible, for a good flavour and texture)
85g (3oz) self raising flour
4 tablespoons amaretto liqueur

APPLE or PEAR TART

Serves 6   Heat oven to 200°C/400°F/Gas mark 6

Butter a 23cm (9") fluted, loose-based tin

Pastry Method

Sift the flour and icing sugar into a bowl. Melt the butter with the water in a saucepan, pour onto the flour and icing sugar and mix to a soft dough. Put the dough into the flan tin and using your fingers, press it evenly to line the tin. Pass a rolling pin over the edges to neaten. Chill in the fridge for 30 minutes then bake blind for 25-30 minutes, until the pastry is browned in centre as well as the sides.

Pastry Ingredients

170g (6oz) flour
2 tablespoons icing sugar
110g (4oz) butter
1 tablespoon water

Filling Method

Peel apples or pears and cut them into medium sized slices. Put into a bowl and mix with the lemon juice and caster sugar. Melt the butter in a large frying pan, add the apple or pear mixture and cook over a medium heat, stirring gently for about 8-12 minutes or until the fruit is tender but not mushy. Using a slotted spoon, take out the cooked fruit and place in the baked pastry case and retaining the juice for the next stage. Put the orange rind and juice into a pan with the remaining apple or pear juice. Bubble for 30 seconds, remove from heat and add the cream and stir. Return to the heat and boil briskly for 1 minute. Spoon this slightly thickened cream over the fruit. Finally, sprinkle the tart with the Demerara sugar. Push the tart out of the flan tin and leaving it on the base, put on to a serving plate. Serve warm or cool but do not chill.

Filling Ingredients

675g (1½lb) dessert apples, pears or apricots
Juice of half a lemon
25g (1oz) butter
60g (2oz) caster sugar
finely grated rind and juice of 1 orange
150ml (5fl oz) carton double cream
25g (1oz) Demerara sugar

BAKEWELL TART

Heat oven to 180°C/350°F/Gas mark 4

8" (20cm) flan tin

Pastry Method

Make the pastry, line the tin, prick the base with a fork and then scatter the halved cherries over the base. Chill while you make the filling.

Pastry Ingredients

170g (6oz) flour
85g (3oz) butter
Pinch of salt

Filling Method

Crumble the sponge and mix with the ground almonds and set aside. Cream the butter and sugar then add the well beaten egg alternately with the sponge and almond mixture. Add a few drops of almond essence. Cover the cherries with the mixture, smooth the top and bake until firm and golden brown.

Filling Ingredients

60g (2oz) trifle sponge
60g (2oz) ground almonds
60g (2oz) butter
60g (2oz) caster sugar
1 egg, well beaten
Almond essence
60g (2oz) cherries halved

BANANA and APPLE CRUMBLE

Serves 4-6   Heat oven to 180°C/350°F/Gas mark 4

Method

Peel and slice the fruit into a bowl, add sugar and lemon juice and mix well. Grease a 2 pint oven proof pie dish and then tip in the fruit mixture. Gently melt the butter. Put the dry ingredients into a bowl and stir in the melted butter until well mixed, spoon onto the fruit. Place in the oven and cook for 30 minutes. If the top looks as if it is getting too brown, lay a loose piece of foil over the top.

Ingredients

100g (4oz) butter
225g (8oz) soft brown sugar
150g (5oz) plain flour
1 teaspoon ground cinnamon
75g (3oz) walnut pieces
675g (1½lb) cooking apples
3-4 medium size bananas
Juice of one lemon
75g (3oz) caster sugar

This topping can be used with other fruit e.g. plums, rhubarb etc. It makes a good crunchy topping which is a pleasant change from the usual crumble.

CHOCOLATE MOUSSE

At Gavin's this was always on the menu and, together with crème caramel, the most popular choice

Serves 6

Method

Break up the chocolate, put in a bowl with the water and melt over a saucepan of boiling water. Stir until it has the consistency of cream and take off the heat.

Ingredients

170g (6oz) plain dark chocolate
3 eggs
2 tablespoons rum or brandy
2 tablespoons water

Separate the eggs and beat the egg whites until stiff, add egg yolks and the rum or brandy to the chocolate and mix well. Fold in the egg whites carefully until there are no white lumps left and pour into individual glasses or ramekins.

Cool in the fridge and top with whipped cream and grated chocolate.

CHOCOLATE and ALMOND TORTE

Serves about 8   Heat oven to 180°C/350°F/Gas mark 4

Takes about 1hour and 15 minutes
24cm (9") cake tin, greased and lined with non-stick parchment

Method

Ingredients

Process the chocolate until it is finely chopped. I prefer to use a large knife as this achieves a better control. Then repeat with the whole almonds. Beat the egg yolks with the sugar and vanilla until it thickens and goes pale. Whisk the egg whites (with clean beaters) to soft peak.

200g (7oz) good quality dark chocolate
4 eggs, separated
175g (6oz) caster sugar
1 teaspoon vanilla extract
110g (4oz) ground almonds
125g (5oz) whole almonds
200g (7oz) butter, melted and cooled to
    tepid
Icing sugar to finish

Carefully fold the chocolate, almonds and cooled melted butter into the egg yolk mixture, lastly, fold in the egg whites. Transfer to the tin, level slightly and bake for about 50 minutes. or until it just becomes firm to the touch. Leave in the tin to cool and then turn out onto a serving plate. To finish, dust the surface with icing sugar. Serve by the slice with a little cream or crème fraiche.

CHOCOLATE SWISS ROLL
with coffee and liqueur

Serves 4 in 4 individual serving dishes

Method

Cut the Swiss roll into 4 slices and place them in the serving dishes. Mix together the coffee, sugar and brandy and spoon it over the Swiss roll slices. It will soak in very well. Top with the cream and grate over the chocolate.

This pudding takes no more than 10 minutes to make and is delicious. I always keep a chocolate swiss roll in the freezer waiting for the occasion when I need a pudding but have little time to make one.

Ingredients

1 chocolate Swiss roll (M&S ones are good)
75ml (3fl oz) espresso or strong coffee
50ml (2fl oz) brandy, rum or coffee liqueur
4 tablespoons caster sugar
4 tablespoons heaped, lightly whipped double cream
or crème fraiche
Grated chocolate

CRÈME BRULÉE

Serves 5-6

6 ramekins or one 1½pint dish/basin

Method	Ingredients
Mix yolks well with the sugar. Heat the cream to scalding point and pour onto the eggs, mixing well. Add vanilla essence. Return to the pan and heat very carefully	4 egg yolks 1 level tablespoon caster sugar 1 pint double cream 1 teaspoon vanilla essence

to thicken, stirring constantly. The mixture must not reach boiling point, unless you want scrambled eggs! Put the dish(es) into a gentle oven to allow the mixture to 'form a skin', but not to colour.

Leave to stand for several hours or in the fridge overnight. Then heat the grill, dust the surface with caster sugar evenly, put the dish(es) under the grill and allow the sugar to melt and brown, then remove and stand in a cold place for 2-3 hours before serving.

This is delicious with fresh fruit salad

CRÈME CARAMEL

This was the favourite pudding of Doreen, a friend of mine, who waitressed on Saturdays and some evenings. When she was serving them she would turn them out onto a pudding bowl and scrape out the last drop. Her sister was married to Derek Nimmo and he was a frequent visitor with Pat, his wife. I always felt he was 'slumming' as he was certainly used to the best London restaurants!

Serves 4-5   Heat oven to 150°C/300°F/Gas mark 2

1½ pint soufflé dish. Instead of a soufflé dish, you could use ramekins. In the restaurant I used to make 24 of them a day (double quantity) it was neater for individual servings.

Method

To make the caramel, put the sugar and water into a medium-sized saucepan and heat gently until the sugar dissolves. Boil rapidly until a good dark coffee colour. Pour into a 1½ pint soufflé dish and coat the base all over.

Beat together the eggs, sugar and vanilla in a large bowl.

Ingredients

275ml (10fl oz) milk
150ml (5fl oz) double cream
4 large eggs
2 tablespoons caster sugar
1 teaspoon vanilla essence

Caramel

110g (4oz) granulated or caster sugar
4 tablespoons water, hot from the tap

Heat the milk and cream to just below boiling point and add to the egg and sugar mixture. Stir well or whisk until well blended, then pour into the soufflé dish. Place in a large roasting tin with hot water round the dish to make a bain marie, cover the dish with foil and bake for an hour. Cool then chill the crème caramel until about an hour before you are ready to serve it. Run a round bladed knife round the edges to loosen, then invert onto a deep plate to serve.

CUMBERLAND PUDDING

Serves 4   Heat oven to 180°C/350°F/Gas mark 4

Butter a 2 pint oven proof dish

Method

Rub the butter into the flour and mix in the sugar. Separate the eggs and whip the whites. Mix yolks together with grated lemon rind and juice and stir into the dry mixture, add milk gradually, stirring well. Finally fold in the beaten egg whites and bake in the prepared dish in the oven for about 25 minutes, or until the top is golden brown and firm.

Ingredients

170g (6oz) granulated sugar
1 tablespoon self-raising flour
15g (½oz) butter
2 eggs
2 lemons, grated and squeezed
280ml (scant ½pt) milk

Do not be alarmed by this runny mixture! During cooking it separates and you end up with a firm crust on top and a soft consistency underneath.

ECCLEFECHAN TART

I went to help a friend who owned a hotel in Grantown-on-Spey. Her arm was in plaster and this was on the menu. – so thank you Isobel for this delicious recipe!

Serves 6   Heat oven to 190°C/375°F/ Gas mark 5

23-25cm (9-10") flan tin

Method

Make pastry in a food processor and use it to line the flan tin.

Whisk sugar, butter and egg together, stir in the vinegar, mixed fruit and walnuts, pour into the pastry case and bake for 40 minutes or until the mixture is set.

Pastry Ingredients

225g (8oz) flour
150g (5oz) butter
50g (2oz) caster sugar
2 egg yolks

Filling Ingredients

2 eggs
175g (6oz) soft brown sugar
110g (4oz) melted butter
3 dessert spoons red or white vinegar
225g (8oz) mixed dried fruit, to
           include some cherries
50g (2oz) chopped walnuts

GINGER and PEAR PUDDING

I don't know where I got this recipe but it has become my most favourite. If I am using too much of the syrup I top it up with a bit of ginger wine, an absolute must for my store cupboard.

Serves 8   Heat the oven to 190° C/375° F/Gas mark 5
25/26cm (10") flan dish

Method

In a small saucepan melt the butter and add sugar and syrup. Bubble away until it is a dark caramel colour then pour into the flan dish. Peel and slice pears, dip in lemon juice and lay on the top, being as decorative as you like.

Blend cake ingredients (but not the chopped ginger) in a blender or food processor then lightly mix in the ginger. Pour onto the pears and bake for 45 minutes. When cool enough to handle, turn out and serve with cream, crème fraîche or ice cream.

Topping Ingredients

75g (3oz) granulated sugar
75g (3oz) butter
2 tablespoons syrup (from a jar of stem ginger)
2-3 pears
Lemon juice

Cake Ingredients

110g (4oz) butter
110g (4oz) caster sugar
75g (3oz) self-raising flour
1 level teaspoon baking powder
25g (1oz) ground almonds,
2 large eggs
3-4 tablespoons syrup (from the jar of stem ginger)
4 pieces of ginger, chopped

ICED GRAND MARNIER SOUFFLE

This was Joan Irvine's wonderful recipe that we used when we opened Ballindalloch Tea Shop together.

Serves 8-10

Method

Ingredients

7 egg yolks
250g (9oz) caster sugar
4 tablespoons water
575ml (1pt) double cream
Zest of 2 oranges – Sevilles are particularly
good if you have a few in the freezer
4-5 tablespoons Grand Marnier

Put sugar, water and orange zest into a saucepan and boil for 4 minutes without stirring. Whisk the egg yolks until thick and light in colour then, whisking all the time, pour in the sugar and orange mixture. Continue to whisk until it has a mousse-like consistency, then add the Grand Marnier. Beat the cream lightly till soft and then fold into the mixture.

To serve, spoon into glass dishes, ramekins or a soufflé bowl and freeze. Remove from the freezer 10 minutes before serving and decorate with segments of orange, all skin removed.

This freezes well but will keep for a few weeks only.

LEMON FLUFF

Serves 6

Method

Ingredients

Cream egg yolks and sugar together till pale and thick, add six tablespoons lemon juice. Dissolve the gelatine in warm water (do not boil or it will be ruined!) and add to the egg

- 3 eggs, separated
- 3 lemons, zest and juice
- 2 level teaspoons powdered gelatine
- 75g (3oz) caster sugar
- 3 tablespoons water
- 3-4 tablespoons double cream

mixture with the grated rind of the two lemons. When this mixture begins to thicken, fold in the stiffly beaten egg whites with a metal spoon and turn into a serving bowl, or individual glasses or ramekins.

LEMON FOOL

Cooking in hot summers, and looking back they seemed all to be hot, was quite an exhausting time. Although we were open seven days a week, we did in fact close after lunch on Sunday. In those days the late Clive Dunn used to come for Sunday lunch with his wife Priscilla Morgan. I was often asked to go later to his house in Barnes where we sat around the swimming pool drinking cool wine. There was always an interesting bunch of people there, but I particularly remember chatting to Elizabeth McGovern. Seeing her in Downton Abbey so reminded me of those days. It was there that I had a couple of puffs of marijuana and felt I was flying. Happily, I got home safely but had some difficulty doing the menu for the following week!

This is a quick and easy pudding, to serve in moments of panic!

Method

Mix together Greek yoghurt and lemon curd and spoon into tall stemmed glasses. Top with grated lemon zest and grated chocolate if you like.

LEMON MERINGUE PIE

It was always lovely when the same people kept returning to eat in our restaurant and gradually I got to know some of them very well. One couple went off to Hong Kong for three weeks and when they returned I had taped Brideshead Revisited for them and they came round to my house on a Sunday night with a bottle of wine to watch it. Virginia Lewis was a researcher with the BBC. She was frequently in for dinner with her friends on her way home and I was often invited to sit and have a glass of wine with them. She sometimes went off on long trips and when I asked her where, she said she was accompanying her mother on a working trip.

It was a year or so later that someone told me who her mother was. Soon after that I found myself doing the Golden Wedding Anniversary for Vera Lynn and her husband Harry Lewis, who was her manager. What an evening!

It was the first time I had ever cooked a whole salmon and charming as she is, told me it was the best she had ever had. Every guest was well known in the music world. She had asked for lemon meringue pie and after the party, I used to make one for her and send it down with Virginia at the weekend.

We have kept in touch over the years and we still exchange Christmas cards.

LEMON MERINGUE PIE

Heat oven to 190°C/375°F/Gas mark 5 - for the pastry
150°C/300°F/Gas mark 2 - for the meringue

Grease and 20cm (8") diameter flan tin

Pastry Method

Pastry Ingredients

Start by making the pastry. Sift the flour and salt into a bowl and rub in the fat until it resembles fine breadcrumbs. Beat the egg yolk and add it to centre of mixture. Bind

150g (6oz) flour
75g (3oz) butter or margarine
1 egg yolk
1-2 tablespoons cold water
Pinch of salt

together with a little cold water. Wrap in cling film and put in fridge for 30 minutes then use it to line the flan ring and bake blind at the higher oven temperature.

Filling Method

Filling Ingredients

Mix the cornflour in a bowl with a little of the measured water. Heat the remaining water in a saucepan and pour onto the blended cornflour, return to pan and

1½ tablespoons cornflour
275ml (½pt) water
1 tablespoon sugar
2 egg yolks
Grated rind and juice of 2 lemons

boil for 3-4 minutes, stirring until smooth. Add the sugar, cool slightly and then beat in the egg yolks, grated lemon rind and juice.

Pour this into the pastry case and smooth the surface.

Meringue Method

Meringue Ingredients

Finally, place the egg whites in a large
bowl and whisk until they reach soft
peak, beat in a quarter of the sugar at

3 Egg whites
150g (6oz) caster sugar

a time, then spoon over the filling and spread it to the very edge of
the pasatry shell, so it seals the top completely.

Cook at the lower setting until the meringue has turned pale beige.
It should be crisp on the outside and squashy within.

Serve warm or at room temperature.

PAVLOVA ROULADE

Serves 8-10   Heat oven to 160°C/325°F/Gas mark 3

Line a swiss roll tin with non-stick paper

Method

Whisk the egg whites until stiff. Keep whisking and add the sugar by the spoonful until it has all been used. The mixture should be firm, glossy and stand up in stiff peaks. At this stage add the cornflour, vanilla and vinegar and whisk in well. Turn out onto the prepared tin, spread evenly and cook for 45 minutes. Unlike meringue, the top will be golden brown and crisp and the centre a little softer.

Ingredients

4 egg whites
225g (8oz) caster sugar
1 heaped teaspoon cornflour
1 teaspoon vinegar
A few drops vanilla extract

Filling Ingredients

275ml (½pt) cream
225g (8oz) fruit e.g. strawberries, kiwi, raspberries, etc.

Allow to cool then turn out onto a clean, dry tea towel. Spread with softly whipped cream and then place on fruit of choice, suitably chopped or sliced.

To roll up, place the Pavlova with the long side toward you, pick up the edge of the tea towel furthest away with both hands and roll the Pavlova firmly towards you. Have a plate ready and roll the Pavlova onto it. This is really easy and looks very impressive.

PLUM FUDGE PUDDINGS

What a simple pudding! But when turned out they look so smart and taste so good. The mixture can be prepared in advance and uses up the leftover plums in your fruit dish.

Heat oven to 200°C/400°F/Gas mark 6

Method

Heat the butter, honey and cream in a saucepan and stir until it becomes a buttery fudge sauce. Put the sugar, spice and breadcrumbs in a bowl and mix well.

To layer

Ingredients

50g (1½oz) butter
1 heaped tablespoon runny honey
2 tablespoons double cream
2 tablespoons soft brown sugar
1 teaspoon ground mixed spice
75g (2½oz) fresh white breadcrumbs
3 ripe plums, halved, stoned and
    thinly sliced

Divide half of the sauce between four ramekins and top with a layer of plum slices and half the breadcrumb mixture. Add another layer of plums and top with the remaining breadcrumbs, spoon over the remaining sauce.

This will happily wait for 24 hours.

When the time comes, place on a baking sheet and bake for 20 minutes, then loosen with a knife and unmould each onto a dessert plate. Serve with cream, crème fraîche or ice cream.

RHUBARB and GINGER CRUMBLE CAKE

Serves 6   Heat oven to 190°C/375°F/Gas mark 5

Butter a 23cm (9") spring-form cake tin and line the base with baking paper

Method

Put the crumble ingredients into a food processor and mix until crumbly. Toss the rhubarb in a bowl with the sugar and ginger. Beat the butter and sugar together until pale and fluffy then beat the eggs in a little at a time, sprinkling in 1 tablespoon flour when you have added about half the beaten eggs to stop the mixture curdling. Sift in the rest of the flour and baking powder and fold in, with the milk, gently but thoroughly. Put the cake mixture into the cake tin, followed by the rhubarb, and then sprinkle the crumble on

For the crumble

110g (4oz) flour,
4 tablespoons caster sugar,
75g (3oz) butter

For the fruit

675g (1½lb) rhubarb, cut into ½"
    lengths
1 tablespoon caster sugar
1 teaspoon ground ginger

For the cake

170g (6oz) softened unsalted butter
170g (6oz) caster sugar
3 eggs
170g (6oz) plain flour
2 teaspoons baking powder
1 tablespoon milk

top. Bake for about an hour: the crumble should be golden and the rhubarb cooked by then and the cake shrinking away from the sides of the tin. Cool for 15 minutes on a rack, then take out of the tin and serve warm with double cream. The cake is good served for tea, and can also be made with other fruits such as pears and blackberry and apples.

TOFFEE TART

This was not only a top seller at Gavin's but a favourite with the waitresses, particularly Suzie. All the puddings were on show on a table and the toffee tart seemed to need slivers cut off quite often to keep it looking tidy

Serves 6

10" tart tin

225g (8oz) shortcrust pastry to line tin - bake blind

Method

Put filling ingredients into a heavy bottomed pan and, stirring all the time, boil till the mixture thickens. Pour into flan case and top with 50g (2oz) chopped walnuts

Ingredients

250g (9oz) butter
250g (9oz) dark soft brown sugar
155ml (5¼fl oz) milk
56g (2¼oz) plain flour

SUMMER PUDDING

Serves 6

Method

Ingredients

Line the bottom and sides of a pudding basin with bread, cut into ¼ inch thick slices, crusts removed.

To prepare the fruit, place in a saucepan and add water and sugar. Cook slowly until the fruit is tender but not mushy and pour into the lined basin. Cover the top with a slice of bread shaped to fit and then stand the mould in a deep plate to catch any overflow. Place a saucer on top and then weigh down with a tin of baked beans or other heavy weight. Pour any overflow back into the mould to help colour the bread.

Chill for 24 hours and then invert onto a shallow glass dish and serve.

Half a loaf of stale bread
350g (12oz) raspberries
350g (12oz) blackcurrants
150ml (¼pt) water
225g (8oz) granulated sugar
450ml (¾pt) custard sauce
Fresh cream, or crème fraîche to serve

Cakes

Every so often we did wedding receptions that were joyous, happy occasions. However, there was one that appeared not so joyous and happy. The wedding cake was delivered earlier and was placed in prime position on my grandmother's lace cloth. When everyone arrived it became apparent that there was an 'atmosphere' and that the families of bride and groom were not going to speak to each other. Just as we were about to serve the lunch it was noticed that the top tier of the cake was at a precarious angle, two of the pedestals were sinking into the bottom layer. We then had to get the bridal couple to come and cut the cake for the photographs before the cake fell to the floor.

It was a rocky start, I hope it ended happily.

BANANA and WALNUT CAKE

My friend Kath told me that she once dropped this cake when taking it out of the oven. She then pieced it back together, topped it with a toffee sauce and it worked so well that she has been doing it ever since.

Heat oven to 190°C/375°F/Gas mark 5

Line two 8" round cake tins with greaseproof paper

Method

Cream the fat and sugar together until light and fluffy. Beat in the eggs with 2 tablespoons of the weighed flour. Fold in the remaining flour, baking powder, bananas and 75g (3oz) of the walnuts. Divide the mixture between the two tins, smooth tops with a palette knife and sprinkle the remaining walnuts on one of the mixtures. Bake for 20-25 minutes until golden brown and firm to the touch.

Ingredients

170g (6oz) butter
170g (6oz) soft brown sugar
170g (6oz) plain flour
3 eggs
3 teaspoons baking powder
3 bananas mashed
110g (4oz) walnuts roughly chopped

Filling Method

Mix all ingredients together well and sandwich the cake together with the filling. Putting the half sprinkled with nuts uppermost.

Filling Ingredients

110g (4oz) cream cheese
1 teaspoon clear honey
Grated rind of 1 lemon

TOFFEE SAUCE

So here is my recipe for toffee sauce.

Heat oven to 220°C/425°F/Gas mark 7

Method

Put all the ingredients into a saucepan and heat gently, while stirring with a wooden spoon. When blended thoroughly, remove the saucepan from the heat and pour over the cake.

Ingredients

175g (6oz) soft brown sugar
110g (4oz) butter
6 tablespoons double cream

Return to the oven at 220°C/425°F/gas mark 7 for about 10 minutes, or until the sauce is bubbling.

CARROT CAKE

Heat oven to 180°C/350°F/Gas mark 4

Line two 20cm (8") round cake tins with baking paper.

Method

Sift the flour with the baking powder, cinnamon and salt. Add the sugar, carrots, nuts and coconut and mix well. Mix together the eggs, oil, milk and vanilla essence and then add to the dry mixture and blend well. Turn into tins, smooth tops and cook for 20-30 minutes, until firm to touch. Cool slightly and turn out onto a wire rack.

Ingredients

225g (8oz) self-raising flour,
2 teaspoons baking powder
1 teaspoon ground cinnamon
¼ teaspoon salt
140g (5oz) light brown sugar,
85g (3oz) walnuts chopped
170g (6oz) grated carrot,
2 tablespoons desiccated coconut
1½ teaspoon vanilla extract,
2 eggs beaten
150ml (¼pt) vegetable oil,
2 tablespoons milk

Frosting Method

Blend together the butter and cream cheese. Add icing sugar and lemon juice. Put a third of the frosting into the cake as a filling and with the remains ice the top and sides of the cake.

Frosting Ingredients

85g (3oz) full fat soft cheese,
60g (2oz) butter
A squeeze of lemon juice,
170g (6oz) icing sugar

CREAM SPONGE

Heat oven to 180°C/350°F/Gas mark 4

Grease and line two 20cm (8") sandwich tins

Method

Ingredients

Warm the milk and butter together gently until the butter has melted. Whisk the egg whites with a pinch of salt until stiff but not dry. Still beating, slowly add the caster sugar and then the egg yolks. Sift in the flour, add the milk and butter and

4 tablespoons milk
1 teaspoon butter
4 eggs, separated
Pinch salt
225g (8oz) caster sugar
170g (6oz) self-raising flour

fold in quickly. Pour into the prepared sandwich tins and bake for about 20 minutes until golden brown and firm to touch. Cool slightly and turn onto a wire rack.

When cold, spread one half with jam and then whipped cream. Sandwich together and dust the top with icing sugar.

Filling

2 tablespoons jam
150ml (¼pt) cream, whipped

When fresh raspberries and strawberries are in season, substitute fruit for jam.

CRUSTY LEMON BUTTER CAKE

Heat oven to 180°C/350°F/Gas mark 4

Grease a 20cm (8") square tin

Method

Ingredients

Put the butter into a mixing bowl and cut it into small pieces. Stand the bowl in a warm place until the butter begins to melt, when it is soft stir in the sugar. Beat the eggs together and stir them into the mixture with the flour. Turn the mixture into the prepared tin and smooth the surface with a palette knife. Bake for about 40 minutes when the surface should be soft, though set and slightly brown.

170g (6oz) butter
170g (6oz) caster sugar
2 large eggs
170g (6oz) self-raising flour
Crusty topping
Juice of 1 lemon
110g (4oz) caster sugar

Remove from the oven and while it is still hot, mix the caster sugar with the lemon juice to make a thin paste. Spread this over the surface. The lemon juice sinks into the surface of the cake leaving the top crispy when it is cold.

Remove from the tin and cut into approximately 16 squares.

EASY CHOCOLATE CAKE

Do not worry about the pouring consistency of the mixture.
It turns out well in the end!

Heat oven to 160°C/325°F/Gas mark 3

Grease and line two 20cm (8") round, straight-sided sandwich tins

Method

Sift the dry ingredients into a large bowl and then make a well in the centre. Add the syrup, caster sugar, eggs, oil and milk. Beat well and pour into the tins. Bake for 35-40 minutes or until the cake springs back when lightly pressed with finger tips. Cool slightly, and turn out onto a wire rack and leave to cool.

Ingredients

190g (6½oz) plain flour
2 level tablespoons cocoa
1 level teaspoon bicarbonate of soda
1 level teaspoon baking powder
150g (5oz) caster sugar
2 tablespoons golden syrup
2 eggs beaten
150ml (¼pt) light-flavoured vegetable oil
150ml (¼pt) milk

Icing Method

Cream together the butter, icing sugar and cocoa powder. Sandwich the cake together with half of the icing and put the remainder on top and smooth with a palette knife.

Icing Ingredients

175g (6oz) butter
175g (6oz) icing sugar
4 level tablespoons cocoa sieved

FARMHOUSE APPLE CAKE

Heat oven to 180°C/350°F/Gas mark 4

Grease a 20cm (8") square tin

Method

Finely slice the peeled apples and place in bowl with the sugar and lemon juice. Stir well to coat the apple slices with the sugar and lemon juice. Leave to stand for 30 minutes.

Ingredients

110g (4oz) butter
225g (8oz) self-raising flour
110g (4oz) granulated sugar
225g (8oz) peeled weight cooking apples
Juice of ½ lemon
1 large egg beaten
¼ teaspoon cinnamon
1 tablespoon Demerara sugar

Rub the butter into the flour until the mixture resembles fine breadcrumbs, then fold in the beaten egg, cinnamon and apple and all the juice collected in the bowl. Pour into the prepared tin, sprinkle with Demerara sugar and bake for 30-40 minutes, until the cake is well risen and golden brown.

Cool slightly then turn out onto a wire tray.

FRUIT CAKE

Heat oven to 180°C/350°F/Gas mark 4

Grease and line a 23cm (9") round cake tin

Method

Cream together the fat and sugar and add the beaten eggs alternately with sieved flour, salt and mixed spice. Mix to a soft dropping consistency with the brandy or rum and the milk, if needed. Fold in dried fruit. Put into the prepared tin and top with the nuts, bake for 1½ to 2 hours. Cool slightly before turning out.

Store in a tin for as long as possible before using as keeping improves this cake.

Ingredients

225g (8oz) butter
225g (8oz) caster sugar
4 eggs
220g (8oz) plain flour
¼ teaspoon salt
¼ teaspoon mixed spice
110g (4oz) currants
110g (4oz) sultanas
225g (8oz) seedless raisins
110g (4oz) glacé cherries
4 tablespoons rum or brandy
Milk, if required
A few halved walnuts or almonds

Preserves

It is some years now since I moved into my new house designed for me by Ken Lawson. Aware of my culinary needs, he made sure that I had a large kitchen and larder. There seemed to be yards and yards of shelves. I was amazed how quickly they filled up. There is satisfaction seeing neatly labelled jams, marmalade, pickles and chutneys in neat rows.

PICKLING VINEGAR

Its always useful to have pickling vinegar at hand to use with freshly boiled beetroot. It is also used for pickling shallots or small onions.

Method

Put everything into a large saucepan, cover tightly and heat gently until on the point of simmering. Remove from heat and leave for 3 hours then strain through muslin. Bottle. It is now ready for use

Ingredients

1l (2pts) malt vinegar
7g (¼oz) blades of mace
7g (¼oz) cinnamon stick
7g {¼oz} all spice berries
7g (¼oz) black pepper corns
7g (¼oz) mustard seeds
4 cloves
1 chilli red or green
15g (½oz) fresh root ginger sliced

161

CAULIFLOWER AND COURGETTE PICCALILLI

This recipe makes a delicious medium hot piccalilli.

2.7kg (6lbs) prepared weight.

Method

Mix together salt and boiling water. Leave to cool. Prepare the vegetables into bite size pieces. Place in a large bowl and cover with the salted water. Leave for 24 hours.

Drain and rinse the vegetables. Mix the turmeric, mustard, ginger, sugar and cornflour together and mix to a smooth liquid with half the vinegar.

Ingredients

1kg (2½lb) cauliflower
675g (1½lb) pickling onions peeled
450g (1lb) salt
4.6l (8pts) boiling water
3 teaspoons turmeric
6 teaspoons dry mustard
6 teaspoons ground ginger
225g (8oz) demerara sugar
50g (2oz) cornflour
1.1l (2pts) distilled vinegar

Pour the remaining vinegar into a large saucepan, add the prepared vegetables and simmer until tender but still crisp, about 20 mins. Stir in the spiced cornflour. Cook, stirring continuously until it comes to the boil and the sauce thickens.
Simmer 2-3 mins.

Pack into jars and cover when cool.

CRAB APPLE JELLY

A few years ago I bought a cherry tree for my garden and was thrilled when after the first year berries appeared in great profusion —but it turned out to be a crab apple tree! Having recovered from the disappointment I am more than happy to have a few jars of the jelly. It is so good with game and venison particularly.

Method

Ingredients

4kg (9lb) crab apples
Caster sugar
Juice of 1 lemon

Wash the apples and remove bruised fruit. Place in saucepan, just cover with water and bring to the boil and simmer until the fruit is soft, about 30 minutes. Pour the pulp into a jelly bag and allow to drip overnight into a bowl. Do not squeeze the bag as the juice will be cloudy.

Measure the juice and pour into a pan. To each pint add 400g (14oz) sugar. Pour in lemon juice. Bring to the boil, stirring gently until the sugar is dissolved, then, bring to a rolling boil for 40 minutes or until a little jelly will set when tested. Pour into small pots and seal tightly while still warm.

GREEN TOMATO CHUTNEY

Method

Chop the tomatoes. Peel core and chop apples. Put all the ingredients except the sugar and a cupful of vinegar into a saucepan and simmer gently, stirring every now and then until the ingredients are soft and the liquid almost evaporated, it will take about 1½ hrs. Add the sugar and the remaining vinegar and stir over a low heat until the sugar has dissolved. Bring to the boil and boil rapidly stirring until thick.

Pour into warmed dry jars and cover when cool.

Ingredients

1.35kg (3lbs) green tomatoes
900g (2lbs) apples (any kind)
2 large onions chopped
110g (4oz) sultanas
1 teaspoon salt
1 teaspoon ground ginger
½ teaspoon ground white pepper
Pinch allspice
340g (12oz) granulated or
    preserving sugar
860ml (1½pts) vinegar

LIME PICKLE

Method

Slice the limes and place in a bowl with salt for 48 hours, stirring occasionally. Toast the mustard seeds for a minute in the oil until they start to pop. Add dry spices and turn them over, then garlic and ginger. Add all the other ingredients and cook gently until the liquid is reduced- this takes 20-25 mins. Cool slightly and pour into warm clean jars and seal.

Wait for 3 weeks before using as this makes a big difference to the flavour. It is very bitter when just made.

Ingredients

12 limes
1 tablespoon salt
2 tablespoons sesame seed oil
1 tablespoon mustard seed
4 cloves garlic crushed
2 or 3 tablespoons ginger finely
    chopped
1 tablespoon ground cumin
1 tablespoon ground coriander
2 teaspoons chilli powder
50ml (8½fl oz) water
250g (9oz) brown sugar
Dash vinegar

PICKLED BEETROOT

Method

Cook the beetroot in salted boiling water until tender. Drain. Cool and peel. If the beetroot is large it may need slicing or cutting into chunks.

Ingredients

Even sized beetroot
Pickling vinegar
(see page   161)
Salt

Pack into jars, add a little salt and cover with the pickling vinegar. It can be eaten almost immediately.

PICKLED CUCUMBER with DILL

Method

Cut cucumbers into chunks without peeling. Put into a bowl, sprinkle each layer liberally with salt. Leave for 24 hours. Put the vinegar into a saucepan, add the dill, mustard seed, garlic and sugar. Bring slowly to the boil, then cool. Rinse the cucumber and pat dry with paper towel.

Ingredients

900g (2lb) cucumbers
Salt
1l (1¾pt) pickling vinegar
    (see page 161)
1 tablespoon dill seeds
2 teaspoons mustard seeds
2 cloves garlic sliced
170g (6oz) granulated sugar.

Pack into jars and cover with the cooled vinegar, adding the flavourings. Seal.

PICKLED ONIONS

Method

Ingredients

To aid the peeling of onions, put them in a bowl and pour boiling water over them. Leave for about a minute then pour off the water, peel, then prick deeply all over with a darning needle. Place the onions in a bowl, cover with brine and leave for 48 hours. Drain and rinse with cold water.

Small pickling onions
Pickling vinegar (see page 161)
Salt 75g (3oz) to every 1l (1¾pts).

Dry in a tea towel then pack into the sterilized jars and cover with pickling vinegar. Do not open for at least 2 weeks, they ideally need 2 months to mature and should keep for a year.

PLUM SAUCE

This is good served with pork, duck and game.

Method

Ingredients

Place sugar and vinegar into a deep heavy bottomed pan and simmer until the sugar has dissolved and half the liquid evaporated. Add the remaining ingredients and cook over a low heat until the plums are soft and the mixture thick 30-40 minutes. Sieve, and pot into the jars. Store in the refrigerator.

275ml (½pt) malt vinegar
110g (4oz) demerara sugar
900g (2lb) Victoria plums
12 whole cloves
½ inch piece cinnamon stick
4 whole star anises
½ teaspoon coriander seeds
Juice of lime lemon and orange
2 shallots finely chopped.

ROWAN JELLY

This jelly can be quite bitter, but I have found that if picked from the tree when the berries are well and truly ripe and about to drop off, the flavour improves immensely. It is very good with venison and other game.

Method

Wash the berries and put into a pan with the apples and just enough water to come level with the fruit and simmer until pulpy. Turn into a cloth or jelly bag and drip into a bowl. An upturned stool is helpful here. Leave overnight.

Ingredients

1.35kg (3lb) rowan berries picked from stalks
675g (1½lb} cooking apples wiped and sliced leaving the core in
450g (1lb) granulated or preserving sugar to every pint of juice
Zest and juice of 1 lemon
Small piece of cinnamon stick.

Measure the juice and add the proportionate amount of sugar. Dissolve over a low heat and add the lemon zest and juice and the cinnamon. Boil rapidly for 15-20 minutes or until a little jelly will set when tested.

Remove the cinnamon and turn the jelly into small pots. Put tops on when cold.

SALTED LEMONS

These lemons are widely used in Moroccan food, they blend in so well with their highly spiced dishes. They are so good with curries and I use them with lots of chicken recipes. If just the skin is used, the flesh can be chopped up and added to rice or vegetables.

Method

Ingredients

Wash and dry lemons and cut through from one end in a cross, as if to quarter them. Do not cut the whole way through but leave the quarters attached. Carefully remove the pips. Add the salt into the lemon and close it up. Press into a sterilized Kilner or preserving jar.

Organic lemons
1 tablespoon coarse salt per lemon
extra lemon juice

Fill the jar to the brim, some juice will come out by the pressure. Add extra lemon juice if required, the lemons must the covered.

Seal and place on a sunny window sill for 2-3 weeks and give the jar a shake every now and again. Then store until required.

SPICED APRICOT CHUTNEY

This goes well with all curries, also cold meats and even cheese!

Method

Put all the ingredients in a heavy bottom pan and bring to the boil. Simmer gently, stirring frequently until soft and thick. This should take about 30 mins.

Turn into warm, dry jars and when cool seal.

Ingredients

500g (1lb) dried apricots
325g (12oz) tomatoes skinned deseeded and chopped
1 large onion, chopped
1 apple peeled and chopped
1 green chilli chopped
1 tablespoon mustard seeds
¼ teaspoon Chinese Five Spice
2 teaspoon turmeric
1 teaspoon cumin
1 teaspoon salt
Pinch chilli powder
2 teaspoons ginger
425ml (¾ pt) white wine vinegar
Juice 2 lemons
325g (12oz) demerara sugar

SWEET RED CABBAGE PICKLE
with CARAWAY SEEDS

This recipe was given to me by Jennifer who started working with B.O.A.C the same day as me. We shared a flat in Richmond overlooking the river until she left to marry a Norwegian. We keep in touch and they have retired to Copenhagen. This Scandinavian recipe is not harsh and is more palate friendly. It goes well with casseroles and cold meats.

Method

Layer the cabbage and onions with salt and leave overnight. In a large pan bring the vinegar, sugar and caraway seeds to the boil for 2 minutes. Drain the cabbage and onion, rinse well and drain again. Add the cabbage and onion to the vinegar and bring back to the boil. Take off the heat, put on lid and leave for 5 minutes.

Ingredients

1.35kg (3lbs) red cabbage, sliced
450g (1lb} onions coarsely sliced
Salt
575ml (1pt) white wine vinegar
285g (10oz) soft brown sugar
2-3 teaspoons, caraway seeds

Pack the pickle tightly in sterilized jars and top with liquid. Seal. This keeps very well.

ST. MARGARET'S, ABERLOUR.